The 10+1 Immutable Laws of Elite Negotiation

Powered by

"The Elite Negotiator™"

Eugeniu Dumitru MIHAI, MSc

Mention of specific companies, organizations, or institutions in this book does not imply they are endorsed by the author, nor does mention of specific companies, organizations or institutions imply that they endorse this book or its author.

All information that is given in this book including, but not limited to internet addresses, emails, or telephone numbers were correct at the time of publishing.

Eugeniu D. Mihai has asserted his right under the Copyright, Design and Patents Act 1988 to be identified as the author of this work.

The 10+1 Immutable Laws of Elite Negotiation is a work of non-fiction. Some names and identifying details have been changed.

Every effort has been made to obtain the necessary permissions concerning quoted copyright material. We apologize for any omissions in this aspect and will be pleased to make the appropriate acknowledgments in any future editions.

Copyright © 2020 Eugeniu Dumitru MIHAI

All rights reserved. No part of this book or any of its contents may be reproduced, copied, modified, or adapted, without the prior written consent of the author

ISBN-13: 979-8639299063
ISBN-10: 8639299063

DEDICATION

To my wife, Aura, and to my daughter, Irina, for being my constant source of inspiration and for challenging me to become as good in negotiation as they (natively) are!

To the memory of my parents, Victoria, and Octavian MIHAI, with more love than mere words could express. Thank you with all my heart for everything!

SPECIAL ACKNOWLEDGEMENT

To my two dearest and closest mentors and friends, John E. Pepper Jr., and Dimitri Panayotopoulos, for their unlimited and selfless support and encouragement shown towards me across so many years. Neither "The Elite Negotiator™" book and training, nor this book would have ever seen the light of the day if it were not for your wholehearted trust! I will always be grateful for what you helped me become and achieve through your constant wisdom sharing!

CONTENTS

	Praise for "The 10+1 Immutable Laws of Elite Negotiation"	i
	Foreword	
1	The Law of *Preparation*	1
2	The Law of *EGO*	22
3	The Law of *Power*	29
4	The Law of *Tactics*	36
5	The Law of *Shoes*	46
6	The Law of *Alternative*	59
7	The Law of *Deadlock*	74
8	The Law of *Total Value*	89
9	The Law of *Expanding the Pie*	101
10	The Law of *Outstanding Communication*	114
+1	The Law of *Reality Check*	126
	My challenge to you, the reader!	131
	The "Elite Negotiator™" Short Nego Preparation Plan	133
	About the Author	139

PRAISE FOR
"THE 10+1 IMMUTABLE LAWS OF ELITE NEGOTIATION"

"**The 10+1 Immutable Laws of Elite Negotiation**" provides the most practical and accessible road map to effective negotiations that I have ever seen.

Eugeniu Mihai draws on a quarter-century of business management experience, including leadership positions at multinational companies like Procter & Gamble, Molson Coors, and the International retail chain Metro Group, to present real-life, personal stories which bring the key principles of negotiation to life.

While focusing on the art of negotiation, this fine book will help any reader acquire the practices and the mindset to achieve sustaining win-win relationships".

John E. Pepper Jr
former Chairman of the Board, President, and CEO
The Procter & Gamble Company

"Another excellent book from Eugeniu. It is short and easy to read and yet full of wisdom with great real-life personal stories to illustrate each of his points. I really enjoyed it and I am sure that you will too! You should also take him up on his challenge at the end of the book which will help you and Eugeniu keep improving!"

Dimitri Panayotopoulos
former President, Vice Chairman & Advisor to the Chairman and CEO
The Procter & Gamble Company

"In today's world, controlling costs is an absolute necessity for any company's survival. Effective negotiation is a crucial part of ensuring optimal costs, and this fact makes this new book from the "guru" Eugeniu Mihai a must-read.

I am ensuring all of my leadership and anyone in a position to negotiate and spend our company's precious monies, is fully versed on the gems of content within."

James Michael Lafferty
CEO
Fine Hygienic Holding Middle East

"Although I went through many negotiations during my 20+ years career working in CPG, Retail, Financial Advisory, Consulting and Foodservice, Eugeniu has the gift to explain the key success factors in an easy to absorb, entertaining and self-effacing way, full of real-life examples and wit.

His negotiation examples reminded me of many of my own negotiation mistakes by not following these **10+1 Immutable Laws**.

I can only highly recommend his book for any negotiator whatever experience level one might have!"

Marc Carena
CEO
Mc Donald's Russia

"Eugeniu's new book is a crisp and refreshing read on negotiation skills. It is rooted in a rich and varied experience. The examples Eugeniu provides illustrate the topics in a distinct and credible way. Eugeniu is an excellent narrator.

Each of the "laws" outlined in the individual chapters can stand on their won. Importantly, they go well beyond negotiation strategy and hold a wider application in business and management. A great read and reference

Hans Dewaele
Member of the Board of Directors, *RJ Brands, Kazakhstan*
Retired Vice-President, *The Procter & Gamble Company*

"Life is an on-going negotiation and, the better prepared you will face it, the better your outcomes will be.

You can apply the **"The 10+1 Immutable Laws of Elite Negotiation"** not only in business but you can also apply them in your daily life: with your family, children, own team. Eugeniu makes it simple to understand these "Immutable Laws" through the day to day cases and real examples that will help to identify yourself in each law.

Congratulations Eugeniu and thank you for making your undoubtful negotiating capabilities available to the rest of the "mortals"."

Javier Garcia del Valle
CEO
Happy Tour Romania, part of FCM Global

"Last year I had the opportunity to attend one of Mr. Mihai's Seminars and based on the personal examples highlighted during the session I was impressed by the speaker's wealth of experience in the negotiation field.

"The 10+1 Immutable Laws of Elite Negotiation" is an amazing guideline for the critical points to be taken into consideration prior to any negotiation.

Even for an experienced negotiator, the book provides a structured approach to any type of negotiation. The detailed real-life examples are a great benefit to anybody considering a carrier in Procurement."

Liviu Raulea
Director International Procurement Middle East and Africa
Marriott International

"Eugeniu's new book, **"The 10+1 Immutable Laws of Elite Negotiation"** is a must read for executives engaged in business negotiations. The book is a practical toolkit that shares with the reader key tricks, tactics and tips to ensure win-win negotiations. It contains many real-world examples told through a creative story telling approach. It is a book that I choose to keep on my desk as a reminder of how to do things right and get the most out of my negotiations. I would highly recommend it for your staff!"

William Dempsey
Chief Procurement Officer *The Ball Corporation*
Former Chief Procurement Officer *Molson Coors Brewing Corp*

"The "10 + 1 Immutable Laws of Elite Negotiation" is a powerful book that will enable people to quickly develop elite negotiating skills. For today's time and attention span crunched world this book is perfect. It cuts right to the heart of negotiating and can get anyone from a novice to a skilled negotiator in record time.

It doesn't matter what job you have or what role you are in, we are always negotiating to improve our organizations, our business, our relationships, and our lives. By understanding how to negotiate well, you don't just improve the well-being of yourself and your organization but those around you – including the people you were negotiating with!

I wish I had it earlier in my career and I'll be recommending it to my students now."

George L. Grody
Former Global Executive *The Procter & Gamble Company*
Current Adjunct Professor *Duke University, Durham, NC, USA*

"Similar to his dynamic and enriching training for so many of us across the Middle East, **"The 10+1 Immutable Laws of Elite**

Negotiation" provides us a "How To Guide" that is so real-world. I especially love his "Law of Preparation" and "Removing EGO from nEGOtiations."

What the reader will appreciate is the enormous gift he is sharing by having collected such rich and valuable experience across both sides of the negotiation table! The book provides rich insight from an expert that has found success across so many unique businesses, functions, and disciplines.

Eugeniu's great book of "real-life" lessons reminds me most about what's typically the key reason behind winning any negotiation. In the end, successfully closing a sale is about our customers ultimately trusting us because of the reputation we earned, the respected relationship we've cultivated, and the integrity behind how we selflessly negotiate. I emphatically agree that we must negotiate "as if we're putting ourselves in their shoes." Well said!

This is a terrific book that will make every smart business leader say that working with Eugeniu Mihai delivers a high Return On Investment. There is not another quick and efficient way to upgrade advanced selling performance! I know it's helping us at Fine Hygienic. Across our commercial teams, Eugeniu had personally helped us better unleash the full potential of our top sales stars across our global team! Thank you, Eugeniu!"

Patrick G. Conklin
Chief Commercial Officer
Fine Hygienic Holding Middle East

"By analogy with the author's rule "4=1" (I will leave the reader to find out himself from the book what this means) I will confine myself to mentioning 4 aspects of my relationship with the author and with the art of negotiation that he is "preaching", plus a small final note.

1. It might have been simple circumstances (or not?) that the author came into my life in two defining moments for me. The first moment, in 2014, soon after being appointed CEO of a relatively large Romanian company (being surrounded by all-new things: new colleagues, new partners, new commitments, luckily not a new market!), I met Eugen during one of his quasi-public negotiation workshops. I liked both the man and the subject so much that I managed to convince him to join me and my management team for dinner. Then I attended his 3-day practical negotiation session together with my management team. Subsequently, I sent most of my key managers to his training. In the following few years, we achieved truly exceptional results with the team (doubling the turnover and market share, 10 fold increase in net profit, a very stable and solid company) and I'm more than convinced that Eugen put two, three "bricks" to the foundation of this success. The second defining moment was in Spring 2020, during the full outburst of the CoVid 19 pandemic. Eugen called me, invested trust in me by sending me the manuscript of his newest book (dedicated to the new generation of business people who lacks time, he said), and asked for my opinion. The moment is significant because we were in full "clash" with the owners of the shopping centers, negotiating who should cover the rent for the lockdown period – a terribly hard subject. I started going through the book, and, to be frank, after the first pages I put on hold everything else I was doing and did not stop until I finished reading it. I jotted down some ideas and I immediately used them in my discussions with my business partners. More "bricks" laid by Eugen to the wellbeing of our company.
2. When I was talking to Eugen about the book manuscript,

he told me several times: <*It's a condensed book, full of shortcuts and relatively simple concepts for today's managers who don't have the time to read anymore "The Elite Negotiator™"* > - his main book that is almost 600 pages long. I answered with reservations, as I am a member of Generation X who spent many days during college and university preparing various projects in libraries. After reading the book, my reservations were irreparably shattered – indeed, this is the best material you could always take with you in negotiations. I do not think there is any form of negotiation that is not covered in this book. Therefore, it is always useful, no matter if you negotiate rents (as it is my situation) or try to persuade your kids to give up eating sweets (another case of mine).

3. I have been asking myself many times why I resonated so well with the author, as well as with the subject. And I think that the answer lays on one hand on the very effective, direct and human way of being of the author (Eugen would say *"But man, the author is really human"* ☺), saying a good joke whenever needed, always smiling, yet each time clearly articulating the objective and the aim pursued – achieving this exceptionally well in writing – his books are very fluent, easy to read, not tiring, despite addressing complicated topics, on the other hand on author's extraordinary experience shared with the readers and with the participants to his training. Inevitably, each of us stumbled over the same issues in our lives as the author and each of us learned or is learning out of these pleasant or less pleasant experiences. And living the consequences too. How good it would have been for someone to teach us before or, to have read this book before doing things, so that we did not re-invent the wheel every time and, thus, minimize the consequences of our mistakes.

4. I am personally a declared fan of "The Law of preparation", "The Law of EGO" and "The Law of shoes". Why is that? Because the outcome of any meeting/negotiation depends entirely on its preparation. And in our day to day work, we tend to skip the preparation because we are experienced people and we think that nothing new can show up to surprise us. And yet, what would the great athletes look like without training? They would look like me, they would not be great athletes anymore. I like "The Law of EGO" because most of the things that do not happen or happen badly or very hardly are due to our too much pride. In fact, someone said that more than 70% of the negotiations that should logically close with a deal fail due to pride. We can also add that over 90% of our decisions are subjective and therefore altered by our internal way of looking at things. "The Law of Shoes"? Because empathy is part of our values. In business, as in life, it is not only about you, it is also about the other party. In fact, Romanians have a splendid saying *"leave room for <Hello>"*. We are guided by this and even if in real life there are "predators, speculators", we minimize them and try every time to keep our partners close.

And my small final observation - I had a quote in the book of Financial Mathematics from the second year of university, I do not remember who said it, but it remained imprinted in my mind. It was around the lines: "who knows how to do business, does it, who does not, teaches others". With Eugen, with his relevant experience, with his many laws of negotiation, this risk is excluded. Have a pleasant reading and, perhaps, take some written notes…."

Dragos Sirbu
CEO
Flanco Retail SA, Romania

"I can highly recommend Eugen's new book **"The 10+1 Immutable Laws of Elite Negotiation"**. As someone who negotiates hundreds of times every week both internally in my organisation and with external suppliers I found the practical advice, recommendations, ideas and problem solving to be valuable and insightful.

The book helps the reader remember the importance of some fundamental principles, challenges the reader to think hard about what success in a negotiation is really about and introduces concepts that will deliver short term wins and long term successes that will endure. It will enable even the most advanced negotiator to improve their skills, use their time more effectively and become a better negotiator. It has done just that for me!"

Andrew Hadley
Western Europe Procurement Director
Molson Coors Beverages Company

"A captivating reading, a text book you could not take a break from reading. Written with deep knowledge, passion and a wonderful touch of real life. I was surprised and honored to recognize myself as a "Samurai" in one of his real-life stories. My over-arching take away is that Eugeniu has a teaching gene in his DNA. Moving forward, I hardly can wait for his next books or rather online sessions. I trust he can be a pioneer of a new approach to negotiations, fully adapted to our current so interesting times."

Cristina Florescu
Former Marketing Director, *Procter & Gamble Balkans*
Marketing Director *REWE Romania*

"We are what we read only if we believe it, apply it, live it. **"The 10+1 immutable Laws of Elite Negotiation"** is a sincere book from an Elite Practitioner of negotiations, with great tips and powerful yet simple tools. Keep them at hand and in your mind and they will save your company and career not only once. Use them daily and your life will be a better one"

Paul Markovits
Vice-President of Marketing
United Romanian Breweries Bereprod (Tuborg Romania)

"Every decade or so, a brilliant writer manages to take on some elusive, unfathomable or otherwise difficult to grasp topic and break it in just the right chunks that make it logical, easy and accessible for the many. It basically levels a mountain which separates the "Elites" from the rest of us, giving the power to the readers.

It's what Eugeniu Mihai does for the Art of Negotiation in this outstanding book. With immutable laws, an Art becomes closer to Logic and Science, not anymore reserved for Artists, but accessible for all. From now on, Negotiation will never be the same, as anyone can become an Elite Negotiator, to the benefit of the "win-win"."

Mihai Barsan
Global Vice-President
International Advertising Association

FOREWORD

The idea of distilling the most important lessons on what really matters when it comes to winning a negotiation had been "cooking" in me for some time. Truth be told, it was ignited by the many questions I have received on this subject from the participants in my "The Elite Negotiator™" training program.

What prevented me from putting them on paper until now was my intention of validating these "***10+1 Immutable Laws***" that I selected, of making sure they are, indeed, the most critical ones and that they work every time, in every negotiation, and they will truly help you WIN!

These "Immutable Laws" cover all critical areas that can make or break a good negotiation: thorough preparation, effective communication, psychology, business strategy, power, tactics, and more. I found these Laws to be simple to understand and apply, yet many of us fail to respect them, and, as a result, we lose deals that we should normally win, should we have respected the Laws. Through my own mistakes and living their consequences, I came to agree with the saying: *"Break these Laws at your own risk!"*

Just like my other book on negotiation, "The Elite Negotiator™", this one too stems from my own, 20+ years-long international business negotiation experience. I tried to make it very practical, easily applicable, spiced as much as possible with relevant real examples and personal learnings from many of my business and personal negotiations, starting at the beginning of my career, a quarter of a century ago, and up until now. You will see those examples in highlighted text boxes and titled "**Real story**". Some of these negotiations were truly challenging, some less so, some were successful, some not, yet absolutely all were full of learnings. Truth be told, the unsuccessful ones were by far a better "professor" for me than the successful ones, despite the "bitterness" associated with them! Therefore, you will notice that I selected to share in this book more unsuccessful negotiations than successful ones. Hopefully, in this way, I will help you avoid making these mistakes yourself!

For reasons easy to understand, I did not give explicit information in my personal examples (with only a few exceptions of positive ones), such that the people, companies or events would not be recognizable, but the essence of the learning is 100% there and true in **all** the cases. **Nevertheless, even if I mentioned specific data in my examples (like prices, costs, etc.), they are all imaginary and have nothing to do with the reality!**

I also tried to keep the book short and to the point, so the readers who have only a limited time, can still enjoy it thoroughly and to the maximum.

I would be very grateful to receive any feedback on this book, on what I should change to make it better via email at eugen.mihai@theelitenegotiator.com

And now, enjoy the ride and all the best of luck with your negotiations!

Bucharest, March - June 2020

1.

THE LAW OF *PREPARATION*

Always prepare like there is no tomorrow, as this is the single, most important factor that will decide your success in the negotiation!

There are no secrets to success. It is the result of preparation, hard work, and learning from failure.

COLIN POWELL
American politician and retired four-star general in the US Army

Success depends upon previous preparation, and without such preparation there is sure to be a failure.

CONFUCIUS
Chinese philosopher and politician of the Spring and Autumn period

I decided to name the first law **"The Law of Preparation"** because I fundamentally believe that the proper, thorough preparation represents the key to success in **all** negotiations, with no exceptions! And that **failing to prepare represents the deadliest mistake one can make in a negotiation!**

The challenge is that I have seen a strong preference in the negotiation community for considering the "strategies and tactics" as the best weapon for winning a negotiation, neglecting the paramount part represented by the preparation. It is totally understandable why this happens: the proper negotiation preparation is a process that, if you do it properly, takes time and effort. Some of the participants in my "Elite Negotiation™" seminars told me that the preparation part does not compare to the glam of the negotiation meetings, as depicted many times in movies, with the participants bluffing, using more or less borderline tactics, deceiving if needs be, to get what they want.

Also, it is true that nowadays many of us look for "shortcuts to happiness" and would like to learn "tips and tricks" that would make us smarter, better, slimmer, etc. And we also look for quick ways to become brilliant negotiators virtually overnight. I remember receiving not long ago a phone call to hold a special half-day training tailored to a sales team. But the brief I received from the General Manager of that company was that the training **must** be focused on tactics and "tricks". They did not want to learn the proper, "hard-working" way; they wanted only the shortcuts. My reply was that it would easier to teach them to become neurosurgeons in half a day, but, no honest trainer would be able to deliver a quality program that would fulfill what he wanted.

I have always said that

More than 75% of the success in a negotiation comes from the high quality of the preparation.

How about the rest that adds up to 100%? The rest depends on how you play your cards and how well you adapt to the dynamics of the negotiation process. I specifically use the word "dynamics" because negotiation is NEVER a static process. On the contrary, it evolves as the negotiation unfolds. So, playing your cards well includes how well you communicate during the negotiation: how well you listen (with your ears, but also with your eyes!!) and how well and how much (or how little!) you speak.

> ### Real story
>
> Now, I would like to share my most memorable negotiation ever. This is the example I give the most: in all my "Elite Negotiator™" training sessions, but also in my speeches on the topic of negotiation. And not because I am proud of it, quite on the opposite... While working in Procter & Gamble Balkans, I was appointed Media Manager for non-TV media across the region. I was very proud of my achievement and about the position. So, I told myself: "What better way to impress my new boss than to strike a super deal?" It was September, the period when the new print media contracts were negotiated for the following year. So, I took advantage of my boss' vacation and negotiated the renewal of the print media contract with the second-largest publishing houses, accounting for almost 40% of the budget.
>
> While I did not do too much preparation (just looking at actual spending in the previous 12 months and the latest update of the need in the forthcoming 12 months) I met the Managing Director of the publishing house and engaged in what was my first real business negotiation. Guess what: the negotiation meeting was over lunch: because I saw it happening in many movies, so I wanted to do it "by the book". It took me a couple of hours, including nice food and some wine, and in the end, I obtained, in my point of view at the time, a super deal: better conditions versus the previous contract (better discount, better ads placement, and improvement in payments terms).

> I was extremely happy and proud when I came back to the office, my head pounding: "WOW, I did it! I am SO good! I am only 2 weeks on the job and look what a great deal I did!"
>
> I prepared the contract and gave it for a signature to the Marketing Director. He congratulated me for the deal, and I was in absolute ecstasy.
>
> The week after, my boss returned from her vacation and I could not wait to brag about my achievement and, surely, I expected her to be as happy as I was. But, to my surprise, instead of congratulating me, she started asking me questions like: "what was the sold-out ratio in the past 12 months for each magazine of the publisher?", "how about the same info about the competitor publishers?", "what was the development of circulation and readership for each magazine across last year?", "how is our page consumption in the magazines of this publisher in comparison with one of our competitors?"... and she continued asking me a dozen other questions that simply made me feel dizzy... In the end, boiling of angriness, she told me in a cold, sharp voice: "you simply did not prepare at all!" I countered, on a soft voice: "but I got a good deal, didn't I?" "How can you know this, without doing the proper negotiation preparation?" – the reply came like a samurai sword.

That was the moment when I realized the importance of truly <u>thorough preparation</u>. And I also realized that, although I got a decent deal, **it was definitely a poorer deal compared to the one I could have obtained, should I have prepared thoroughly!** And, by the way, I was grateful that I was not fired after such a stupid mistake!

In all my "Elite Negotiator™" training, workshops, and speeches I always have one slide on which I write an equation that I ask the attendees to look at and write it on the back of their eyelids, so, when they close their eyes, they can still see it!

min 4 = 1

Then I tell the attendants that if there is only one thing, they will take away from my presentation it should be this equation. But what do I mean by that strange equation? It pictures that you must take the proper amount of TIME to prepare the negotiation. Actually, take lots of time! It is said that **one needs to invest 4 times more time in the preparation than the expected meeting time.** In other words, if you expect to have 4 hours of meetings, then it is advisable to prepare for at least 16 hours. It is clearly not a science or a "pharmaceutical" approach, but it is proven that the **longer you prepare, the better off you will be.**

I do hope I convinced you, dear reader, of the importance of the negotiation preparation. Now I can hear your question: **"OK, you convinced me, but HOW DO I PREPARE?"**

That is a great question! To which the answer is not an easy one, but I will briefly take you through the key areas you MUST consider when preparing ANY negotiation. And while the space of this book does not allow us to elaborate on each step of thorough preparation, I strongly encourage you to read Chapter 2 of "The Elite Negotiator™" book, which takes a holistic view of the areas you MUST cover when preparing. You will see that Chapter 2 takes more than half of the whole book, which is another testimony to the importance of the proper preparation.

So, what should we look at, when preparing a negotiation? Here are **4 quick tips that will serve you well:**

TIP #1
Do an outstanding Due Diligence on the company you are going to negotiate with and their people.

> *Diligence is the mother of good fortune.*
> BENJAMIN DISRAELI
> British politician of the Conservative Party who twice served as Prime Minister of the United Kingdom.

First, let me clarify what "Due Diligence" means: as per the Cambridge Dictionary, **"Due Diligence is an action that is considered reasonable for people to be expected to take in order to keep themselves or others and their property safe."** When applied to business, the same source says: **"Due Diligence is the detailed examination of a company and its financial records, done before becoming involved in a business arrangement with it."**

I like to say that "Due Diligence is what you must do before lending a large amount of money to someone". In other words, would you lend a significant amount of money to someone without thoroughly checking the person's background and credit standing beforehand? Well, do the same in business!

It is important to mention that **you must perform Due Diligence both on the company you will be dealing with AND on its representatives!** I will share with you some key things to do and consider in order to be better prepared.

For the company, I am listing here some key areas where you must look (depending on your specific case you may have additional areas, but these are mandatory irrespective of the specific business):

- **what is their business health status?** Look at the way their

P&L evolved in the past 3-5 years. Pay special attention to the topline (=revenue): how much is the "ordinary revenue" as a percentage of total revenue? The ordinary revenue is the revenue obtained from the main activity. It is also known as "organic revenue". For example, if you are selling cosmetics, organic revenue is the one obtained from the sales of cosmetics. If your company obtains revenue from other sources, for example from renting some unused property, then that revenue is called "extraordinary revenue". A significant amount of a company's revenue MUST be organic (ordinary). It might be needless to say, but you must also check any relevant mass-media articles on the company and its business evolution.

- **get feedback from other companies that worked with them:** do they fulfill all their contractual obligations all the time? I always like to ask the potential suppliers to list some of their current business partners that I could reach out for references. Here please make sure you ask them to respect the GDPR Data Protection regulations and only share with you the respective personal data after receiving the consent of the people!
- **what is their financial health?** Do they have outstanding credits? I always ask for their financial statements: Profit & Loss Account and the Balance Sheet, for the past 3 years. If possible, I check the free cash flow statement too. And while I check these statements for the potential suppliers myself, for the important ones I always ask a more thorough check performed by my colleagues from Finance & Accounting.
- **are they paying all taxes to the state?**
- **how do they comply with the Anti-bribery, Anti-corruption (ABAC) standards?** Do they have business/personal relationships with government officials?

Ideally, prepare an ABAC questionnaire and ask their legal representative to answer and sign it. Watch out if the company you are checking has any personal relationships with government officials. In that case, involve your legal / compliance department to advise and give clearance before closing any deals with that company.

While these might scare some of you, let me give you some good news: there are companies specialized in such assessments and you should simply buy the report(s) from them. There are many, but here I would like to mention one that The Molson Coors Brewing Company is using to analyze the stability and "health" of a potential business partner: **The Dun & Bradstreet (D&B) report**. The D&B report is like a personal credit report but for the business operations and is issued by the credit reporting agency Dun & Bradstreet. It gives you valuable information about a company, including creditworthiness, financial stress analysis as well as credit scores that assess the future solvency of the company.

Real story

I was running a tender for car leasing services and I invited all the major players from the country. I did the thorough Due Diligence for all of them and one particular company (let us call it "Smart Car") looked "shaky" in the D&B rating as well as in the financial health reports. Still, I did not exclude Smart Car from the tender, so I sent them the technical brief too.

When analyzing the offers, to my surprise, the best prices for our request were from Smart Car. Frankly speaking, I was hesitating whether I should get a special approval for this supplier (because of the shaky rating) or not... But when going deeper, I understood that their pricing was faulty! In my interpretation, they were pricing low to win market share fast.

> While this is a tactic that I have seen done countless times, the effect it had on the P&L of Smart Car was not good! They were losing money for 3 years in a row! So, whatever market share they "bought" via their low pricing was NOT SUSTAINABLE! How did I come to this conclusion? If it were sustainable, Smart Car could have started to increase their pricing for their existing clients – and this would show in the P&L.
>
> After the full analysis, it was clear to me that I will not recommend Smart Car! It would have been much too risky for a contract that is minimum 5 years long! And, to nobody's surprise, all my Board colleagues agreed with my recommendation to go for the next best offer from the tender, although it was a bit more expensive, but had better overall total value.

For the company representative(s) please make sure that:
- **they are entitled and empowered to represent their company in the relationship with you and your company.** Can they take commercial and legal commitments on behalf of the company? Are they still working for that company? Don't be surprised by this last question: I know the story of a Managing Director of a large Romanian printing company who still claimed in front of his suppliers that he is working there, while his contract ended several weeks before. Imagine that he could have signed a deal with a supplier, although he was not entitled anymore. So, it is good advice to ask the necessary clarification questions, nicely and professionally, such that there will be no hurt feelings. To give you a personal example, when I worked for Procter & Gamble Balkans, I was employed by Procter & Gamble Romania, who had the power of attorney to act as a service provider for the other countries outside Romania.

Otherwise, I would not have been legally entitled to negotiate for my projects outside Romania!

- **you do a background check on them.** The simplest way is to start with our dear friend Google. It will give you plenty of information to start with. Then ask around in your business network. People's reputation (be it a good one or a bad one) is something that spreads around, so you will easily find out if there are alarm signs regarding them.

Real story

I will give you now a personal example when I got into troubles because I did not do my proper due diligence when preparing to negotiate.

One Fall, I had an incident with my house: the heating pipes broke after I turned on the central heating. The house was 5 years old (so practically new) and covered by a 10-year warranty against hidden defects by the law. So, I took a lawyer and we went to the company that sold us the house (let us call it "Big House Seller") to negotiate my compensation. We met the Managing Director of Big House Seller, as well as their lawyer. While we expected to encounter resistance, we were very confident about our odds. After all, we did very well our homework: we studied the law, we had extra-judiciary expertise after the incident, proving the hidden nature of the defect, and we estimated all damages and so on. We tried to negotiate with them 2 times and in both instances the representatives of Big House Seller were inflexible.

So, we went to the next step, which is going to court. The court proceedings take a long time in Romania, so I spent approx. 2 years until the final verdict came. And there was the biggest shock of my life because we lost the lawsuit! How could it be

> possible? Well, on a small technicality, but big enough to make me lose a lot of money. What was the technicality?
>
> The company I bought the house from did not build the house! They had a contractor who hired the building company, the electricity company, etc. In other words, I took to court the wrong company! Should I (and also my "great" lawyer) have investigated the legal position of the seller of the house, we would have identified the issue. The bad news is that, after losing the initial lawsuit, I could not start a new one against the responsible party because of the time frame of starting a legal action versus the moment you discover the fault is maximum 6 months... while I found out about the technicality 2 years after the incident. So, here it is how an improper preparation can ruin the whole negotiation and make you lose a lot of money...

When doing the background check of the people you plan to negotiate with, try to find a connection point (hobby, the countries they have been, same friend, etc.) to immediately increase the personal touch in negotiation and break the ice.

It is important to mention that **Due Diligence is even more important during a crisis**. The best example is the Global pandemic generated by CoVid 19 and the ripple effect it had on the World economy. There was hardly any economic area that was not affected by the CoVid 19 crisis. Some areas have been more affected than others, but the impact is clearly broad-based. Some areas collapsed almost entirely, like the travel industry, some were less hit, as the food retail, others even grew, like some pharma areas.

But, to be extra sure and safe in such turbulent times, I strongly recommend that in all cases, before starting any negotiation, you **do a much more thorough Due Diligence than you would normally do**. Do it for both the company you will be negotiating with, as well as for the people that will be representing it. Ask for proofs of financial stability from the other side and, if feasible, ask for guarantees of payment and/or delivery. And, if you are buying, avoid as much as possible the advance payments, especially in the case of the small suppliers. Work out with your Finance and Legal departments the best ways to protect your company if things go south. Mark my words: **in crisis, there is no such thing as too much background check!**

TIP #2

Clarify your objectives in the negotiation and what are your limits for each of them.

There is an old saying: "If you don't know where you are going, any road will take you there". The same holds in a negotiation: you must know what your objectives are, their relative importance, and what are your limits for each objective. And, by the way, make sure you stick to those limits in the heat of the negotiation!

There are two types of objectives in any negotiation: in other words, two key interests:

a. **the material objectives (interests).** These are the things you want to achieve from a commercial point of view, for example, price, payment terms, delivery terms, warranty, service levels, etc.
b. **the relationship objective (interest).** Here we look at whether you want to have a long-term relationship with the other party or not.

There is always a conflict between the two objectives! The more you push to obtain the material objectives, the less you will be able to obtain in the relationship area. And vice versa. And therefore, it is difficult to be very tough when you negotiate with a good friend (here the relationship interest is very strong).

When thinking of the ways to achieve your objectives, remember to balance the short-term interests with the mid/long term ones.

While this may sound so obvious and quite easy to apply, I have seen countless times people (including myself!) unable to respect it. Why is that? Quite simply because we are, in most cases, literally chased to fulfill the short-term objectives. We need to deliver the sales volumes, the profit margin, the cash flow, as well as many other specific KPIs for the current month, the current quarter, or the current fiscal year. If we fail the short term, there might be no mid or long term. Neither for the company nor for us!

For example, in Procurement we too have many short-term targets: Cost Savings, Cost Avoidances, Non-recurring cost reductions, Cashflow improvement (Days Payable Outstanding), and many more. And we became more or less "slaves" of the short term because every month we must report the progress against all these short term KPIs.

Do not get me wrong! There is nothing wrong with having short terms KPIs, in fact, it is mandatory! But, alongside the short terms KPIs you must know the vision of the company as well as the KPIs for the mid/long term. By the way, the mid/long term KPIs should be the same as the short term KPIs! Once these are clarified, you will be able to jot down a glide path of getting to the vision KPIs starting from today's KPIs. You decide the KPIs for each following year, then break them down as appropriately by quarter and by month.

Balancing the short and long term involves many decisions that you must make. Let me tell you something that you might not realize immediately, but it is sobering true: **ALL decisions we make create precedents for the future!** No exceptions! Today's decision will impact the mid/long term, one way or another. The important question we must ask ourselves is the following:

> **Do we create a positive precedent with this decision?**

As much as possible, try to create positive precedents! They will make your life significantly easier and your related decisions in the future will be greatly helped by this positive precedent. Think of it as the Butterfly Effect!

One more particularly important point I want to raise here:

> **When deciding on a course of action, always be very clear on what trade-offs you make between the short and mid/long term**

Are you comfortable with them? If yes, go ahead. If not, what issues do you spot? Are there ways around them? Consult with your upper management and see whether they can agree on a different set of priorities that would make better sense. Or align with your bosses any compromises you will have to make in the process, what KPIs you will not be reaching 100%, short or mid/long terms

I will give you an excellent example of a company who managed very successfully balanced the short and long term:

Real story

I was negotiating the car service contract for our company car fleet with the top 8 largest providers of operational leasing and fleet management. They were all multinational companies, with excellent track record and reputation.

The best value was offered by a company that was in the top 3.

> It was not the cheapest offer, however the overall value they offered was excellent. One thing that surprised me was the relatively modest management fee they requested. It was not awkwardly low, but it was below what we received from everyone else. So, I was determined to understand what they had in mind by making this pricing decision.
>
> In our final meetings, I asked them about the pricing strategy for their fee. They were extremely open and replied: "We only wanted to cover our costs. We did not want to make any profit out of this contract. But what was important to us was to get your company as a client in our portfolio and at the same time offer more work to our partner car services around the country. Their survival, especially in these tough times (this took place during the CoVid 19 pandemic crisis), is critical for us mid-long term."

So, this company balanced the short-term need (covering their operational costs) with the mid-long-term objective: ensuring another reputable client in their portfolio AND helping their partners around the country. Simply brilliant strategy!

Unlike this company, many of its competitors in that pitch proposed quite high management fees – reflecting their clear short-term interest.

I want to talk now about one more thing: the way multinational companies think their management assignment lengths (2-3 years per assignment) encourages the bad habit of the job holders to think much more short-term vs long term. I have seen many cases like this in my career in P&G, METRO Group, or Molson Coors. And if these managers are incentivized by short term bonuses, with little or no equity (company shares that mature mid/long term), then a deadly combination is achieved!

So, what to do if you are in such a situation? I think it boils down to each person's ethical standards: do they commit to doing the right thing for the long term or not? You cannot force people to care for what is right, I am afraid! But I have been blessed in my career with a mix of both short and long term assignments. Two of the longest lasted 12 years! Honestly, when I accepted them, I did not even dream that I would perform them for such a long term! And you can imagine that, if I were not doing the right short term / long term balance, I could have never succeeded to deliver at the level I delivered (and became a Best In Class example across the region) for those many years.

This also reminds a quote from the famous Spanish singer Julio Iglesias, who started singing over 52 years ago and who commented on his 5 decades-long success: *"You can't fake it for 4 generations, you must do it from your heart!"* Yes, I completely agree with him: doing whatever you do from your heart is the only way to achieve long term success!

TIP #3
What is your vision of the ideal WIN?

I have a particular interest in discussing this because throughout my negotiation career and during my negotiation workshops and seminars, I have seen people truly obsessed with WINNING in negotiation. Winning was everything for these people – they wanted it all and they wanted it every time! They would go to great lengths to achieve (all) their objectives, many times making compromises that they should not have or do things that would not be normally justified.

All this insane quest for "WIN no matter what" made me reflect on "what is really WINNING in a negotiation"? Is it gaining the maximum possible out of the negotiation, as most of the participants in my training answered when I asked them this question? Or is it preserving the relationship at all costs? Or rather balancing in the best way the material interest with the interest for the relationship? How about achieving the perfect implementation of the agreed deal? But what about making the other party crave for negotiating again with you? Or even recommending you as an example of an ethical and fair negotiator? And I could go on like this for much longer...

So, what is really WINNING? Is there a simple answer to this question? For many people, unfortunately, there is. And for these people, the answer they gave me was "I win if I gain as much as possible (materially speaking) from the negotiation". What do YOU think, dear reader? Take a minute (or two) and think about YOUR past negotiations. About what you achieved and how. About how happy (or unhappy) you and the other party were AFTER the negotiation. About the implementation of the agreed deal: how did it go? Was it fully implemented, as per agreement? Or the other party (or even you) did not fulfill all obligations? How about the relationship you had with the other party AFTER the negotiation? I guess you need more than a minute or two to think about these questions... And I guess by now you have already realized that the answer to the question "how do I win in negotiation" is much more complex than it looks like at a first glance.

I will share in the following paragraphs my thoughts on this matter. I have personally applied these ideas in many negotiations; therefore, I believe they will add value to you too.

Winning is achieving a negotiation result that lies within the boundaries you set for yourself when you prepared.

For example, if you set an interval between 10,000 and

13,000 USD for a car that you want to buy, ANY value within this interval is a WIN! I know you feel like there is a "bigger" win if you buy the cheapest possible (10,000 USD in our example), but the scope of setting the limits during preparation is exactly to avoid this so-called "post-deal remorse".

> **Winning means preserving (or even improving) the relationship with the other party AFTER the deal is implemented.**

Yes, I hear you saying: "This is true for win-win deals, but what about "one-time deals"?" Indeed, for those, the interest in a relationship is minimal. But, please, do not leave the other party to feel they were robbed! Do it with courtesy and "leave the door open" for the future. There is a saying that the world is small, and you never know when the roads will cross again with the other party. Try to make the other party crave to return to the negotiation table with you for another deal – even talking to others about how professional you are!

> **Winning means the sustainable implementation of the agreed deal.**

I have seen too many times the "fake win-win approach". What is this? It is when I claim to act as "win-win" but I only care about my "win". I do not want to crush the other party, but I do not work hard enough to ensure he/she truly wins as well. The acid test for this is the implementation phase. If the other party did not win, then the implementation will be lousy and below the agreed standards. And if you find yourself in this situation, I will dare to say that you actually LOST the deal!

> **Winning also means giving up a deal if it is not going to work for you!**

Now you are probably shocked: "What is this?" "How come a "no-deal" is WIN??? Well, when I bumped into such a situation, I had the same normal questions as you have now. But then, thinking over, I realized that it is true: if you agree to a deal that is NOT fully satisfactory to both of you (or is fully satisfactory only to one of the parties), then you will see it fail in the implementation phase. This partially satisfactory deal is happening mostly when one or both parties do not have alternatives – hence they settle for a mediocre result – which for sure will not be fully implemented. So, my STRONG advice is twofold: a) always have a (strong) alternative and b) say NO if the deal is not the right one for you or the other party. The other party will thank you for the honest approach – I can bet all my money on it!

So, after debating these several facets of winning a deal, you must make your own decision: what type of WIN do YOU want from your next negotiation? I know this seems complex, but if you always think about "acting on what you believe to be true" (quote from John E. Pepper), then you will find the answer that best serves you. One thing for sure: winning never means "grabbing as much as possible with both hands", like many people, unfortunately, think and act while pretending to be having a win-win strategy

---

TIP #4

Put together a plan to achieve your objectives. And wisely and smartly stick to it!

I would advise you to approach the negotiation preparation systematically and fill in a Preparation Plan. You must cover things like your strategy, tactics, power sources, alternatives, persuasion techniques, etc. In "The Elite Negotiator™" book I am sharing a comprehensive Negotiation Preparation Plan that will serve you well in your toughest dealings. For the quick and simpler negotiations, (but without being sloppy!!), I have designed a shorter version of the Preparation Plan. I present it at the end of the book, and you will see that it includes the absolute minimum amount of info you must consider before entering ANY negotiation.

Before ending, I will share with you another personal example, this time a positive one! It is one of the negotiations I worked most preparing for, but the result was great!

Real story

I was negotiating with an agency their fee for the dedicated team allocated to us on a special project.

We requested the agency fee to be expressed in terms of direct costs, overheads, and profit margin. When we got the quote, we were quite surprised, as it was quite high. Taking out the overhead and the profit rate (that we knew in terms of percentages), we were left with quite a big amount of direct costs. We knew the team structure (no. of people allocated to the job and the percentage of their time used in our projects), but we could not know the exact salaries for each person due to confidentiality. So, we had to do very thorough research to estimate these individual salaries by looking into specialized salary surveys done by the HR community and business magazines. This was quite tedious work and required us to do a lot of mathematical simulations. But my Purchasing colleague and I rolled up our sleeves and did all the needed computations!

Next, we told the agency that the agency fee was way too high for our budget and asked them to propose another team structure, considering that we may have fewer projects (thus asking them to eliminate from the team some members). They reverted with another team scheme, with fewer people, and with another cost, lower than the first one, but, still too high.

We started analyzing the new scheme, inserting our salary assumptions. To our surprise, we saw that we were overcharged. In the new agency structure, with fewer people, the decrease in fee was too small vs the decrease in personnel! So, we asked for a clarification meeting with the agency.

Here is how we did it, using the "Salami" strategy: in the meeting with the agency, we started by validating our assumptions regarding how they pay their people (labor contract versus private company). Once this was confirmed by the General Manager of the agency, we put on the table, in front of him, the two scenarios of teams: the initial one and the reduced personnel one. And we pointed out that the decrease in direct cost was way too little, hence we do not understand how the computation was made. To save face, the General Manager, after turning into all rainbow colors, told us that he must go back in the agency and look again into the numbers. In the following week, he came back to us with a more reasonable and fairer fee proposal and we finally signed the contract.

The learning? **Thorough preparation really pays out!** Should not we have done the digging into the salary surveys and shouldn't we have done all those simulations, we would not have any solid argument why we were overcharged. It cost us more than a week of work, but the result was truly worth it!

And one final advice: always keep in mind that:

"TODAY IS THE TOMORROW YOU DIDN'T PLAN FOR YESTERDAY!"

2.

THE LAW OF *EGO*

Always forget the EGO when negotiating, as it will harm you in countless ways!

The worst disease which can afflict executives in their work is not, as popularly supposed, alcoholism; it's egotism.

ROBERT FROST
American poet

The weak are dominated by their ego, the wise dominate their ego and the intelligent are in a constant struggle against their ego.

HAMZA YUSUF
American Islamic scholar and co-founder of Zaytuna College

I do not know if you noticed this, but the word **negotiation** has the word EGO embedded in it!

n**EGO**tiation

Is that a coincidence? Or perhaps not? We will never know…

But what we know for sure is that the EGO is a real killer

when it comes to negotiations. In my opinion, allowing your EGO in a negotiation is the **second-largest mistake you can make**, after the lack of preparation (that we covered already in *Law of Preparation*).

Do you remember the story I told you in the *Law of Preparation*? The one regarding my first business negotiation? I was a real "champion" then because I not only did the biggest negotiation mistake, but I did also the second-largest mistake: I had a HUGE EGO!

Paraphrasing Albert Einstein, **"the product between EGO and knowledge is constant"**, or, in other words, the more EGO you have, the lesser the knowledge you possess and the other way around.

Always remember that the negotiation is not about your pride (or EGO); it is about you obtaining the maximum result possible. And for this, you need to think clearly, objectively, and without being blinded by emotions. And, ideally, humbly! The best negotiators I have ever seen were humble people, suppressing their EGO and making sure they put reaching their targets as their number one priority.

I love giving the example of Lieutenant Colombo, magically played by the late Peter Falk. He was looking so strange, behaving odd, and many times talking self-deprecatingly. The suspects never took him seriously until it was too late. He knew how to play "dumb", how to "caress the EGO" of the suspect, to make him lower his "guard" and talk too much, giving away precious information. Colombo simply looked helpless in many cases; you felt sorry for him and you wanted to help him past that awkward state. But no, behind this look there was the sharp mind of a world-class detective who never missed any detail!

I strongly recommend you buy the Integral Series of Colombo and watch every movie. I guarantee you will learn a lot.

There is even a negotiation tactic called "Colombo" simply because it asks you to behave like the famous Lt: sometimes a bit helpless, clumsy, forgetful, admiring the intelligence of his counterpart. OK, but just do not copy him 100% because you will be caught, and you will make a fool of yourself. Just add touches of his behavior and invite the other party to show how smart he/she is!

I need to admit that it is not easy to play Colombo. Why? Because of our EGO, which tells us how smart we are, how good we are, how "Center-of-the-Universe" we are.

Let me share with you now a real story that highlighted so well to me the importance of (not having) an exacerbated EGO.

Real story

I was invited to hold a special seminar about the "Fundamentals of Elite Negotiation" to a large labor union. The participants were leaders of labor unions from various cities. Besides being a truly enjoyable and interesting experience, I came to realize that the union-management negotiations do not really have alternatives. Or, better said, there is no positive alternative. From the union side, the only alternative is the work conflict (which can be escalated to labor strike). If the conflict/strike happens, then all parties lose: the management will lose the production for the conflict/strike period, while the union members will not get any pay. So, the two parties are somehow "married" together. At first glance, one might say that there are strong grounds for finding a mutually acceptable solution, right? Not necessarily so. Dare to guess why? Well... in many cases, EGO plays a big role – on both sides.

> In my seminar, I had 2 simulations involving labor union-management negotiations and none was closed! Both ended up in deadlock – which means, in real life, that a work conflict was born due to the incapacity of the parties to come up with a decent solution. In addition to the EGO, the labor union did not prepare properly – they demanded salary increases, more benefits, etc. but had no reason why; they just claimed that the people need these, without giving to management grounds for accepting the demands. The management side (in the simulations played by the union members) acted from a position of force, with very few concessions and an inflexible attitude. After debriefing, I was told that the two simulations resembled the real ones more than 90%!!! In addition, at the end of the seminar, the participants said that it would be great for management if they would attend my training as well.

Before going into some personal advice on how to "tame your EGO", let me share with you some highlights from a recent interview with Sir Anthony Hopkins that are spot on this topic:

> *"We are not special. We are just ashes at the end. The EGO is the most dangerous part of us. EGO is the enemy! You must have a little bit of it to keep moving. But you let it go out of control, then you become a power freak! You see it in the papers every day. The corruptness of corporations, their greed, their power, their belief they are gods. And they all reach damnation in the end. We have to pay the price for our actions!"*

Now, as promised, let me take you through a simple, yet highly effective **4-steps approach to keep your EGO under control.**

1. **Acknowledge you have an EGO problem.** I know I am not saying anything new, but without your honest, deep acknowledgment that you HAVE an EGO problem, nothing can be done! As Sir Anthony Hopkins said, some EGO is good it is mandatory to help us progress. But, like anything in life, when something positive is too much, it becomes dangerous. To make a joke, I give you the example of water: water is vital for life. Without it, we die. Yet, too much water is detrimental; it is called "drowning" …
But how to see if you have an EGO problem? Very simply! Ask for feedback from people who know you, who care about you and your wellbeing. You may not like what you hear, but certainly, you must do it if you want to change.
2. **Commit to change.** Once you have acknowledged the EGO problem, next you must make a commitment, a vow to change. And KEEP IT! Do not be like those who start very committed a diet and drop it after a few days/weeks! It is a lifetime commitment, because unlike in the case diets, the EGO problem affects many more people than just yourself, THROUGHOUT your lifetime!
3. **Learn to listen truly effectively.** While we will cover effective listening in the dedicated *Law of Outstanding Communication*, let me just say here that listening is crucial in negotiation. It is the ONLY WAY for you to get information from the other side. And here I'm talking about the information that the other side gives you voluntarily, but also the information that you get indirectly (for example by observing the speech pattern of the other side, by listening beyond words, by listening to information that the other side gives you to fill in the silence, etc.). In a nutshell, there is nothing like too much or too good listening!
4. **Do not just focus on yourself.** EGO means exactly

"focusing on oneself" because one believes he/she is the most important person in that respective relationship or conversation. Focusing on YOUR needs is mandatory, of course! But if you do not pay attention to the other side's needs, problems, pain points, how are you going to convince him/her that what you are offering is the best for his/her needs? It is "putting yourself in the other party's shoes" – as we will discuss in the dedicated *Law of Shoes* later in the book.

So, in conclusion, if we want to obtain a significant advantage in negotiations, we must forget all about our exacerbated EGO! It will not work easily from the first trial, especially if you already have a big EGO… Therefore, I recommend that you start little by little, following the 4 steps indicated above. Just like following a diet or going to the gym, once you see the positives of this approach, your confidence in yourself will grow, and you will become a better negotiator.

Only one final watch-out: do not over-do it and suppress your EGO fully, so the other party uses you as a mop to wipe the floor! Just keep it at a normal level and, if the other party crosses the line, make sure you remind them about the good business practices!

3.

THE LAW OF *POWER*

Always make it a priority to maximize your negotiation power by leveraging your strengths and exploiting your counterpart's weaknesses!

Nearly all men can stand adversity, but if you want to test a man's character give him power.

ABRAHAM LINCOLN
The 16th president of the US

Power is not an institution, and not a structure; neither is it a certain strength we are endowed with; it is the name that one attributes to a complex strategical situation in a particular society.

MICHEL FOUCAULT
French philosopher, historian of ideas, social theorist, and literary critic.

A Jedi uses the Force for knowledge and defense, never for attack.

MASTER YODA
Star Wars character

It has been proven again and again that there is a direct correlation between the level of power a party has in a negotiation and the outcome of the meeting, with the caveat that one needs to "play the cards in the best way!". What do I mean by this last sentence? I would say that it is equally important how much power you have and how well you use it to serve your purpose!

Before we dig into details, I would like to underline two particularly important aspects regarding Power:

---

1. If you believe you have Power, you are right; if you believe you do not have Power you are also right.

This is a paraphrase of a famous quote from Henry Ford I, but as true today as it was over 100 years ago when it was said. Most people underestimate their power level and do not feel confident enough because they are very aware of their limitations. But I will tell you something: your counterpart is not a mind-reader, so he will not know ALL your limitations, as well as you know them. So, do not undermine yourself unnecessarily. Remember that the power you have starts first with what is inside your head!

---

2. In a negotiation, bargaining strength depends on the <u>perceived</u> level of power you have.

In other words, if the other party believes you have power, then you have. The reverse also holds: if you do not make the other party feel you have power, then you do not have it!

When preparing for a negotiation, you must ask yourself **5 important questions**:

1. How much power do I have?

Here you must brainstorm on all possible sources of power and evaluate your strength for each of them. But, to properly prepare, we must understand that we can draw power from two main sources: **from us as individuals** (and I will call this as of now on **"Personal source of power"**), but also **from the company** that we represent (if it is a business negotiation). It is critical to look at both sources of power and see what traits we can use as power elements to help us in the negotiation.

I want to pause a little and talk about the impact the **Company power** has on us. Working in large multinational companies for over 20 years I took for granted the fact that I represented Procter & Gamble, real,- Hypermarket/METRO Group, or Molson Coors. And when I had successful negotiations, I thought that my "outstanding" negotiation skills granted the wins. How wrong I was! In many cases, the **Company power** had an extraordinarily strong impact on the negotiation outcome; I would even dare to say that in some cases it was critical for success. But I did not realize this at the time! It was easier for my EGO to think that I was the "artisan" of those great deals… So, my "cold shower" advice for you, dear reader: if you represent a large company, be realistic and do not get drunk with plain water! If you are successful in your negotiations, be grateful to your employer first, then pat yourself on your back for your negotiation skills! You will realize I am right when you will run your first negotiation **without** having a large company behind you! You will be surprised how small your power will become in comparison to the power you used to have when your large employer was backing you up.

In Chapter 2.12 of "The Elite Negotiator™" book, I describe at length **46 sources or types of power.** You will see that some of them can be drawn from us (**Personal source of power**), some from the **Company** and some **from both.** If you feel that a certain source of power would be useful to you in the negotiation, then think about how you can get that power. Let me give you one example: if you believe that the power of expertise would positively influence the outcome of the negotiation in your favor, but you are not an expert in that field, maybe it is worth getting an expert to join you in the negotiation. Most likely your counterpart is not an expert in that field either, so having a true expert on your side will help a lot.

One more thing: by no means, I have exhausted the possible sources of power in my book! I only listed the ones I feel are most common, most used, and sometimes quite easy to have. Obviously, there are other sources as well, so please feel free to add to that list.

At the end of this chapter, I will be sharing my personal top 10 sources of power, as well as the way to get/leverage them in the negotiation.

2. How much power does the other party have?

During preparation for the negotiation, you must evaluate not only how much power you have, but, using the same algorithm, to estimate the power of your counterpart. Go through the list of power sources and put yourself in the shoes of the other side. I know this will be a difficult process because you do not know what is in the other party's head. Also, you might not get it all perfect from the first try but persevere and you will see the benefits shortly.

3. How can I increase my power to maximize the negotiation result?

Think about what the weak points of your counterpart are and try to find strengths (power sources) for you in those areas. This asks for incredibly good preparation and knowing extremely well the other side (do a proper SWOT analysis by the way and you will see it paying off!)

> **Real story**
>
> I remember that, when I was Media Manager in charge of non-TV media buying for Procter & Gamble, many times publishing houses would come to see me and propose that the company enters with advertising in their new magazines that were about to be launched on the market.
>
> Normally I would not accept because, in a case of a new magazine, you do not know beforehand what readership and circulation they will achieve, so it is impossible to calculate an accurate cost per reach point.
>
> So, I could easily say NO and refuse to enter. And I did this in several cases of magazines published by no-name publishing houses that had no previous success in this area. For the other publishing houses, however, my approach was different. I knew they needed Procter & Gamble for two reasons.
>
> First, because Procter & Gamble represented an endorsement or a vote of confidence in the new magazine. Most of the other advertisers would buy advertising in a magazine if Procter & Gamble is present there.
>
> Secondly, Procter & Gamble had money, hence the magazine

would be helped in a period of cash flow problems due to high launch expenses.

So, how does the power analysis look like in this case? Well, the magazine has a weakness in terms of money, and they needed the "vote of confidence" from Procter & Gamble – these would be critical for a good start in business. And these were exactly Procter & Gamble's strengths!

As a conclusion, in each such situation, I agreed to advertise for 3-4 months after launch (or until the readership data were issued), but I negotiated extremely good prices, with much bigger discounts versus the regular contracts. In this way Procter & Gamble's risk of investing in a new magazine was compensated by a better price – therefore the risk of loss, if the magazine would be a flop, was minimized.

4. How much power should I use?

This is not an easy question, because if you have power but you underuse it, then you may obtain less out of the negotiation than you would normally deserve. On the opposite, if you overuse the power that you have, you may end up gaining more from the deal but damaging the relationship.

Abuse of power has always been detrimental to long-term relationships, hence, if you employ power tactics, be careful at the balance between maximizing the gain and maintaining the relationship. In one of my groups, one student asked me the following question: "but what about the distributive negotiation? For example, if I am negotiating to buy a car, I have no real interest in the relationship, so I can overuse my power as I see fit, right?" What do you, the reader, think? I believe there is no right or wrong answer if you keep yourself in the line of ethics and you do not feel ashamed of your behavior.

One more particularly important point regarding power:

Power is not something fixed throughout the negotiation, but it is DYNAMIC!

Because of the bargaining process, which includes exchanges of information, dialogue, and re-assessment of the situation by each party, the balance of power may shift one way or the other. So, do not "sleep" happily knowing that you have a strong position at the beginning of the negotiation – this can change very fast and you will "awake" suddenly! Be alert and re-estimate the power level for both you and the other party regularly, taking any corrective actions needed to re-increase your power level.

While I cannot describe at length all 46 types of power, like I did in my "The Elite Negotiator™" book, I am hereby listing, as promised, my personal **Top 10 sources of power** and a short description of each.

Nr.	Power source	How to get/leverage
1.	**Reputation**	A critical source of power, greatly enhancing your credibility and trust. Build it by always keeping your commitments and doing this every single day!
2.	**Financial**	Having financial strength (both personal and at the company level) generates power in the negotiation. At a personal level also creates peace of mind – important for being "clear-minded" when making decisions.
3.	**Integrative (win-win)**	Starting with the win-win mindset and maintaining it throughout the negotiation process is the most powerful weapon you can use to maximize the result for both parties. It builds

		trust between the parties and shows a genuine desire to reach mutually satisfactory results.
4.	Precedent	Precedent power is very strong, and it works in many cases because everything we do creates a precedent. Use it in your favor by searching for similar precedents.
5.	Perseverance	Do not give up after one NO! Come again with your argument, ideally from a different perspective. Understand the objections, answer them, and come again with your argument.
6.	Information	The more information you have on the other side and on the negotiation subject, the higher power you have.
7.	Investment	There is a direct link of proportionality between the time you invest in a relationship/negotiation and the amount of compromise you are willing to make. So, get the other party to invest time and resources in the relationship with you and you will have stronger power in the negotiation.
8.	Competition	Create a competition for what you offer (e.g. by organizing tenders), and you will strengthen your BATNA.
9.	Principle	Having a set of sound personal and business principles is highly recommended because it is helping you make the right decisions every time. And, when doing so, you have as a compass the set of principles (in Procter & Gamble we called this "Principle-based decision making", or "PBDM").
10.	Persuasion	The stronger you are in influencing and persuading the other party, the higher chances you have to obtain a good deal.

4.

THE LAW OF *TACTICS*

Always use the negotiation tactics as tools to support your strategy, not as a replacement for the strategy!

Strategy without tactics is the slowest route to victory. Tactics without a strategy is the noise before defeat.

SUN TZU
Chinese general, military strategist, writer, and philosopher from the Eastern Zhou period

Tactics involve calculations that can tax the human brain, but when you boil them down, they are actually the simplest part of chess and are almost trivial compared to strategy.

GARRY KASPAROV
Russian chess grandmaster, former world chess champion

Before we start, I would like us to align on what the term "tactic" means. A usual dictionary definition is **"an action or method that is planned and used to achieve a particular goal"**. The word **tactic** is allegedly said to have been used for the first time in 1640, although it originates from the Greek word *taktikē,* (the feminine of *taktikos*).

I have noticed a "passion" for negotiation tactics, both from the part of trainers and book authors, but also from the side of those learning the negotiation art. In all my negotiation training, everybody was waiting anxiously for the chapter about tactics, like they would represent the "golden secret" of becoming a great negotiator. I believe that a negotiator must know the tactics very well because this is how he will recognize them when used by the other party and will be able to properly counteract them. But focusing exclusively on learning the tactics will NOT automatically grant the upper hand in the negotiation. By comparison, the thorough preparation (which includes the selection of the tactics to be used) will put you in a significantly more advantageous position.

I have written several negotiation articles for different business magazines and delivered negotiation-related speeches at conferences. In both cases, I was asked to share "tips and tricks" or "tactical shortcuts" to "win in the negotiation". In my speeches, I always say this: "do not ask me for the magic formula to win in a negotiation, because there is none except **the thorough preparation**! Tactics will NEVER replace your lack of preparation! Not ever!". Some of the people did not like that I was destroying their fantasy, but many of them got the point. Unfortunately, some kept on believing in the 'shortcut to happiness". By the way, I strongly encourage you to watch the movie "Shortcut to happiness", starring Anthony Hopkins, Jenifer Love Hewitt, and Alec Baldwin. I guarantee you will learn an especially important life-long learning – **there is no free shortcut to happiness**!

When considering using a specific tactic, always ask yourself the following questions (I call this list of questions **"The acid test for using negotiation tactics"** because you must pass the test of EACH question if you want to use the tactic safely):

1. Will I feel ashamed if the biggest selling newspaper would put on the front cover a story describing me using this tactic?

This is also known as the "New York Times rule", and to me, it represents the most important question you must ask yourself before using any tactic. I know that there are people out there who do not care about their public image! But I hope that most of the people reading this book care, so I am telling you again: do anything that will make you feel proud if the World will know about what you've done!

2. How is this tactic fitting my ethical principles?

Your actions will speak louder than your words. You may claim yourself as an ethical person, but if you employ borderline or plainly unethical tactics, THESE will define who you are in the eyes of the others, not your words!

3. Is this tactic fitting my overall negotiation strategy?

The use of any tactic must be congruent with the overall negotiation strategy you have chosen because, as said, tactics are supposed to SUPPORT your strategy and help you win.

4. Is this tactic fitting my usual negotiation style?

You must take care that the selected tactics are not shocking to the other party, especially if you did business with him/her before. Nobody likes to have surprises – we all prefer to work with people we can predict, so do not create surprises. Act in your usual negotiation style. And this is valid not only in cases of behaving tougher than your normal style! I always had a question mark on people who behaved too well in negotiations. The "too nice to be true" behavior only made me more alert.

5. What alternative tactic I can use if this one is not working?

This is an important question because you must proactively prepare if your first-choice tactics fail.

6. How is the other party going to react to me using this tactic?

What would be my response to their reaction? Do not think the other party will simply sit there and say yes to your tactic. In 95%+ of the cases, the other party will reply with a counter tactic. So, think which one is most likely to be used?

The points 5. and 6. above resemble very well the Chess game: ANTICIPATE your counterpart's reactions and moves and foresee the best responses for each potential situation.

In Chapter 2.16 of "The Elite Negotiator™" book, I am sharing the details of the top 80 negotiation tactics. Just like in the case of the sources of power, the list is not at all exhaustive. But the list includes, as said, the most widely used tactics. Please beware that **not all 80 tactics are ethical and by no means, I endorse all of them!** But we must be acquainted with all of them, may them be ethical, borderline, or outright unethical, so we can defend against the borderline or unethical ones and leverage to our advantage the ethical ones.

While the space of this book does not allow me to present at length all the 80 the tactics I mentioned above, I have selected 10 that I consider **The Top 10 ethical tactics**. Here they are, together with a brief description for each.

Nr.	Tactic name	Brief description
1.	Barter	Use other forms of compensation than money for what you buy/sell. It can be Full Barter (use 100% compensation other than money) or Partial Barter (part of compensation is money, the rest being something else of value to you).
2.	Acceptance time	Do not reply immediately to a proposal, even though you might know you cannot accept it. Take time to think about it. It also shows respect vis-à-vis the other side. Also called Consideration Time.
3.	Backburner	If you get in a deadlock over one subject, postpone it for later. In this way, you may reach agreement on other points and in this way, help reach the agreement, later, on the one causing the deadlock too.
4.	Ask open-ended questions	Ask questions that cannot be answered with Yes or No, but with details, so you get information. Ex: Why?, What?, How?, When?, Where? etc.
5.	Flexibility	Show flexibility within the range of your limits, do not stick to fix positions.
6.	Auctions	Create competition for what you are buying by tendering potential suppliers. There are various types of auctions: Dutch, English, Japanese, Reverse, Sealed bid, etc.
7.	Identification	Reassure the other party that you understand his/her problems and that you want to find a win-win solution. Shows empathy and builds

		trust and positive relationships.
8.	**Last & final offer**	Use it when you reached the limit for the subject you negotiate. Do not exceed it unless having a serious reason, or else you lose credibility.
9.	**Patience**	It helps you think more clearly, gain time to think, and make the best decisions.
10.	**Straw issues**	Issues that are not at all important to you, but you use them (pretending they are important) in exchange for issues that truly matter to you.

I will share with you one of my favorite real examples, a negotiation that brilliantly shows the power of the **Barter**.

Real story

When I organized the Spring Anniversary event for the retail chain I was working for, I had a very limited budget. Nevertheless, I had the ambition to organize an event that will be great, especially that it would have been the last one prior to the company being purchased by another chain.

So, I decided that I want to organize a raffle with prizes for customers, but also one for employees of all the stores and of the headquarters. As "big prize" I wanted to give luxurious one-week all-inclusive vacations in a foreign country.

I contacted a large travel agency and asked the CEO to give me a quote for the trips. I negotiated the price quite strongly and I got a decent discount.

But the total cost was way above my budget... what to do?

The CEO of the agency proposed lower quality hotels, such that we fit in the budget. Clearly, that could have been a solution, but not for me. I wanted excellent quality for our customers and employees, so I did not accept the offer. I took some time off to think about what can be done.

> Then I realized that the CEO mentioned his low advertising budget... and an idea came to my mind: what if I do a partial barter? The travel agency wants TV advertising but cannot afford it. We will do TV advertising for this campaign, so why do not I add them to my spot as "main partners of the event" and request them to pay me in "trips", not in money.
>
> I met the CEO again and I made this proposal to him. He agreed and then we started the bargaining over how many trips and how much media exposure we would offer them.
>
> In the end, we obtained all the trips we wanted, at a great discount, while the travel agency got their TV exposure (as a bonus I put their logo on all our in-store posters and all printed materials).

Once you get accustomed to all the tactics, the next challenge is to decide what strategies and tactics you will use in the forthcoming negotiation and to estimate what strategies and tactics the other party will employ. After you decided your strategies and tactics, for each of them you must think what the other party will say or do (in other words, what will be the counter-tactics of the other side). It is very much like the chess game: you estimate the reaction of the other side for each of your moves.

But I already hear your question: **"HOW shall we select the tactics?"** I will give you some personal advice, based on my extensive experience in this field:

1. Always select ethical strategies and tactics

It is easy to say but for some people not so easy to implement, especially that it is so easy to lie or misrepresent the facts. The acid test is the "New York Times rule" that I mentioned earlier in this chaper: **"How would I feel if my tactic would be exposed in primetime on the biggest audience TV station? Would I be ashamed or not?"** I remember a very recent situation when, in negotiation gameplay, although the instructions for each participant were truly clear and specific, one participant immediately started the negotiation with a big lie about a big offer that he presumably got. I still do not understand why he did it…

2. Put yourself in the shoes of the other party when you employ the tactics

What would be your reaction if the other party would use that particular tactic? Would you feel comfortable using the tactic? If you would not like that tactic to be used on you, then do not use it yourself either!

3. Use those tactics that you feel comfortable playing

This is especially important advice because you must be credible when using a certain strategy. If you look like reciting a poem, then you do not have much credibility.

4. If your counterpart uses unethical tactics, call them by name

This is one of the most effective countermeasures for unethical or borderline tactics because you expose the maneuver and the other side will highly likely feel like a thief caught in the act. In most cases, the other side will stop the undesired behavior.

I will give one more example of a real situation, this time describing a time when I caught someone using a dirty tactic called "Deliberate mistake". In a nutshell, this tactic means that you insert a mistake in your proposal, a mistake that favors you. You hope that the other party does not discover it (or at least not until it is too late). If the other party discovers it, then you can pretend it was a simple mistake.

> ### Real story
> Procter & Gamble was planning a big broad-scale sampling program across the country and I was the leader of that project. Following a bid, the sourcing team selected one agency to perform the project implementation (let us call the agency "Time Agency").
>
> When I got the detailed cost estimate from Time Agency, the total cost seemed a bit too high. I met the agency together with a fellow Purchasing colleague and we looked through the detailed cost estimate. Without bragging, I tell you I am good with numbers, so it rapidly struck my eyes: in the cost estimate, there were some costs added twice, hence the inflated overall cost.
>
> I showed this to the owner of Time Agency in the same meeting and she immediately blushed and apologized for the mistake. I can bet all my money that she was very well aware of the "mistake" and, in fact, that was a "deliberate mistake". After that moment I never was able to trust Time Agency again.

In closing, always remember that **tactics are only TOOLS to help you get a better deal.**

They are NOT the substitute for sloppy preparation and will not save your deal if you did not do your homework!

5.

THE LAW OF *SHOES*

Always put yourself in the shoes of the other party!

Always put yourself in others' shoes. If you feel that it hurts you, it probably hurts the other person, too.

Rachel Grady
American film director and producer

You just need to put yourself in someone else's shoes and then see how they feel and then you will understand why they are reacting or why they are behaving the way that they are behaving. We need to be fair.

Navid Negahban
Iranian American actor

This law is of particular importance because it can help you gain a significant competitive advantage in your negotiation, should you apply it properly and consistently. Why am I saying this? In my personal experience, there are **three key reasons to use the approach** of putting yourself in the other party's shoes.

In all three situations, it is of paramount importance that **one side deeply understands the other side**. Let us take these cases one by one and discuss them:

REASON #1
When you want to understand better the other party's needs and pain points
Known also as **The Iceberg Theory**

Like icebergs, people normally expose only a small part of themselves, and generally, just the part they wish to show.

NIKKI YANOFSKY
Canadian jazz-pop singer

I always try to write on the principle of the iceberg. There is seven-eighths of it underwater for every part that shows

ERNEST HEMINGWAY
American journalist, novelist, short-story writer, and sportsman

Humans are not easy persons to be understood. In many cases, I was faced with people that normally should have agreed with me in certain negotiations, but to my surprise, they did not. It seemed illogical at the time. I was thinking: "How can it be? Why is he not agreeing? It's obvious that it's an excellent solution for him as well".

What I was missing to understand was the fact that not all the **interests** or **positions** or **motivators** of the other party are openly shown to the other party or easily visible in a negotiation. Nobody will tell you that he will be fired if he is not signing the deal with you! But, in reality, it may very well be so.

Before diving further, let us spend a few minutes to clarify the three particularly important terms that I mentioned in the above paragraph: **interests**, **positions**, and **motivators**. These are not at all the same thing, although many people confuse them, so let us tackle and clarify them one by one:

- **Interests** (also known as **issues of the negotiation**) refer to **the concrete areas of interest for both parties in the negotiation**. Examples:
    - rental price per square meter,
    - the length of the lease contract,
    - delivery terms,
    - maintenance terms, etc.

  The two parties must take quality time to discover and align ALL interests or issues to be negotiated. This is always done at the beginning of the negotiation, to make sure that nothing important is left out. I mentioned earlier in the book (in *The Law of Preparation*) that there are two major interests in any negotiation: **the interest in the material aspects** and **the interest for the relationship**. I also said that these two interests are always conflicting: the higher is the interest in one, the more difficult it is to maintain a balance of the other.

- **Positions** refer to **specific conditions or offers** for each issue. Taking the same examples as above, here are some examples of positions (in **bold** fonts):
    - rental price: **5 Euro per square meter**,
    - the length of the lease contract: **2 years**
    - delivery terms: **30 days after receiving payment**
    - maintenance terms: **24/7 service on all weekdays**

- Unlike issues and positions, which are material, **motivators** are psychological needs, feelings, or desires. You also need to know that, for the same person, motivators may change over time if background factors change.

> The "Iceberg" principle in negotiation states that in most of the cases, only a small part of information about the other party is easily visible (the "tip of the iceberg"), while the bulk of the information is hidden.

You must search and dig for that hidden information because only addressing that part properly you will finalize easier and better the negotiation. This "iceberg" principle uses the analogy of the iceberg, where you only see ca. 10% of its volume, the rest (90%) is underwater.

The "tip" of the iceberg normally consists of the material needs or wants of your counterpart (e.g. money, goods, services, material outcomes of the negotiation, etc.). By contrast, **the bulk of the iceberg is usually represented by the psychological needs (or better said "motivators")**.

Examples of motivators: desire to be liked, to be appreciated, career advance, pleasure, a good image in front of others, recognition, keeping the current job, having an easier life, etc. Exactly because they are psychological and hidden, they are difficult to be spotted. The figure below tries to suggest the "Iceberg Theory" in negotiation:

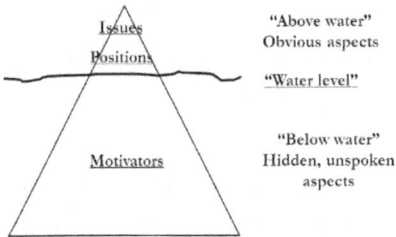

As a matter of fact, if we want to be scientifically precise, **there are only two fundamental motivators in life for all**

humans. These two motivators drive all our actions. Scary, isn't it? Think about yourself: why do you do what you do? List all motives before reading further. Can you group them in clusters? Did you end up with two groups? Yes? Then you are absolutely normal, do not worry!

The two main motives for all our actions are:
- the need for pleasure and
- the avoidance of pain.

And, by the way, they are exactly the key reasons why somebody would negotiate with you. Don't you believe me? Think again. Why do you work? Most likely because you need an income. Why do you need income for? Food? Housing? Vacations? These fall in either of the two buckets.

But exactly because they are psychological needs, **they are extremely important for the person and he/she will not spell them out for you**. You either find them or not – and if not, you lose in the negotiation.

My advice is to spend quality time to understand the hidden drivers of the other party and to see how you can satisfy them. You will be able to make exchanges later during the negotiation process by offering satisfaction to the other party on some of their psychological needs, in return for obtaining important material or psychological needs for you.

Always focus on the issues AND on the motivators, as it is the only way to reach a mutually advantageous result in the negotiation

---

Now that we understood the psychological background of our actions and motivators, let us see how we can apply these practically.

The secret of successful selling a good or service is to understand better than anyone else the needs of the buyer. It is as simple as that! I like to call this "the doctor's approach".

I tell everyone attending my training the following story: imagine you are not feeling well, and you go to your doctor's. And imagine that, as soon as you enter his office, he hands you the prescription with your medication, without you even having the chance to open your mouth to tell him what is hurting you! I can bet you would be startled, truly perplexed. Going past the initial shock, my key question is: would you take any of the pills he prescribed you? I bet all my money that you would never do it! Why is that? Because **he did not listen to you to understand what is bothering you!**

So, I think we have an understanding: you would not take pills that were prescribed without the proper understanding of your health status. Now I have one very tough question to you, dear reader: if you agree that medicines must be prescribed based on a proper consultation, why do you sell things without the same deep understanding of the buyer's needs? Just because we are not talking about health, but a simple sale, it does not mean that we should have a different approach!

When I was Business Development Director in an advertising agency, I was told that I must get appointments at potential clients and present them the agency credentials, which included all types of services that the agency was offering. I followed that advice for some time, with moderate success.

One day, however, I decided to test the "shoes" approach. Here is a small, real story on my first "shoes" approach:

Real story

I struggled quite a lot to get an appointment with Joanna, the Trade Marketing Manager of a very large multinational company (let us name the company "Beautiful"). So, I was determined to make the most out of this unique opportunity!

I went to the meeting without my usual "gear", I mean without my laptop; I only had a notepad and a pen. In the meeting, I could see a bit of a strange look on Joanna's face. For sure she thought I was a strange breed... taking notes on paper, with no laptop...

After the usual warm up chat, I looked in her eyes and I asked her directly: "Tell me, Joanna, what's keeping you awake at night?". Her eyes widened. I immediately added with a smile: "from a business point of view, obviously!" I could see her relaxing. I continued: "what challenges are you currently facing for your brands?" And I asked my favorite question: "If I were a fairy and I could grant you 3 wishes (business related), what would those be?"

All this time, I was taking detailed notes about what she was telling me. The conversation lasted short of one full hour and I had about 3 A5 pages full of notes. I summarized my take outs to make sure I got everything right, then I told her very bluntly:

"I'm here to help you sleep better at night by helping you fix your business where it hurts. Based on what you just told me, I can confirm that our agency is able to help you with issues number 1, 3 and 5 from your "pain" list. I am afraid that, for the issues 2, 4 and 6, we do not have the expertise at a level that would make us stand out in front of our competitors. Next, I will send you within 3 days a tailor-made proposal outlining how we can help you. For the balance of your "pain points", while I cannot make any promises, I will think of other agencies that

> would be able to help you better than us." Here she was perplexed: she said that she never saw an agency representative being so "no-BS" and straightforward, let alone to recommend competitors!
>
> My reply was instant: "We want to truly help you. If I lie to you now by overselling our capabilities, you will see the reality quickly and our reputation will be ruined. Our collaboration will be a short one, for sure. So, why on Earth would I ever trick you into buying something that's not helping you??"
>
> Long story short, "Beautiful" became an agency client and the collaboration was anything but a short one! And all thanks to the approach: honest, transparent and client focused!

After seeing the success of the "doctor's approach", I not only used it as of then with all clients and potential clients, I also trained my peers from the agency to do the same. But, in all honesty, it was a very difficult paradigm to change, because, for years, the "established approach" was to go to the potential client and flood him/her with everything that you can do, no matter if he/she needs only one type of service.

One of the trickiest negotiations had always been the one between a salesman and a retailer buyer. We all heard how tough the buyers are and how difficult it is to "please" them. I have been requested recently to hold a training for the senior sales team of the largest paper producer in the Middle East. One of the points I was briefed to cover was related to understating the needs of a retailer.

I am sharing here below, in a nutshell, the main ideas from my speech, with tips that you can successfully apply with any retailer, even with the most stubborn one!

Real story

Across the years, I have been negotiating with many retailers, some local, but most of them international. I have done it representing giant corporations like Procter and Gamble, but also very small, entrepreneurial companies. I also worked for over 3.5 years in retail, so I saw the buyers "at their home". Therefore, I was lucky to have multiple data points that allowed me to distill important conclusions about what a retailer needs. I am sharing here what I learned from these experiences.

A retailer usually wants two things: **Increase in turnover** and **increase in profit** (ideally both **profit margin** and **absolute profit**). To note, some may want **market share** as a priority!

Going back to what we just learned (the "doctor's approach"), we must think how we can help the retailer achieve these objectives:

- **_Increasing Turnover_**. The Turnover equation for a retailer is the following:

$$Turnover = ABS \times USh \times FV$$

where

ABS = Average Basket Size,

USh = Unique Shoppers

FV = Frequency of Visit

Increasing Turnover can be achieved by increasing any of the 3 members of the turnover equation (or 2 of them or even all 3). To summarize, here is how you can achieve turnover increase:

$$\uparrow Turnover = \begin{cases} \uparrow Avg\ Basket\ Size & = \uparrow VALUE \\ \quad or \\ \uparrow \#\ Unique\ shoppers & = \uparrow TRIAL \\ \quad or \\ \uparrow Frequency\ of\ visit & = \uparrow LOYALTY \end{cases}$$

Next, assuming that you sell the Brand M, think how can M increase the basket size by increasing its value? Or how can M increase the trial for that particular retailer (= make shoppers chose that retailer to the detriment of the other competing retailers)? Or how can M increase the loyalty for the retailer by making the shoppers come more often to that store chain?

• **Increasing Profit.** Think how can your Brand M increase the profitability of the category? Either as percentage (=profit margin increase) or as absolute profit. Or both.

• **Increasing Market Share.** Just like for profit, think how your Brand M can help the retailer gain more market share.

You can see that, while the retailer diagnosis might seem complicated, it is amazingly easy if you put yourself in their shoes and understand what they need!

I would like to underline that putting yourself in the other party's shoes to understand better his pain points and needs is not to be used solely if you are a salesman! You must use it in <u>any</u> negotiation, but also, if you are a marketeer, to understand (better any competitors) the needs of your target group! I know this is basic stuff and everyone is talking about the need to do it. But the question is: *"are you doing it day in and day out, are you true to this commitment of understanding the needs of those who buy your brands and ultimately pay your salaries?"* I remember a video broadcast with the Chief Marketing Officer of Procter & Gamble at the time, Jim Stengel. At the beginning of the broadcast, we could see Jim entering the studio walking very funny, almost stumbling. Then, after he sat in his chair, we could see that he was wearing high heels (I even remember their color: deep red!) He wanted to talk in that broadcast about understanding women (as a key target group for most of Procter & Gamble's brands) and he wanted to make the point about walking in your consumer's shoes. What an effect this had, as I still remember this after many years!

REASON #2
When you want to understand better the impact of your actions on the other side

I know that you may lift an eyebrow upon reading the above. Not many people care very much about the impact of their words or actions on others, or at least not on every occasion.

One of the most important qualities of a leader (but I would say that this must be valid for any person) is how much he/she CARES about the others. CARING makes a huge difference between being successful in rallying people around you, having them happily follow you, come Hell or high water, or being a "lonely wolf" who struggles to make up a team.

Is caring important in negotiations? A big YES from my side! Even if it is a short-term deal, showing that you understand the impact of your words and actions on the other side can only benefit you. And you will be both short term, in that very deal, but also longer-term, through the impact on your reputation.

So, as a conclusion, it is very much worth the effort of understanding (beforehand) what the impact of your actions and words will be on the other side. So, please make this effort and put yourself in the other party's shoes and think about what YOUR reaction would be. If you do not like how you feel, then reconsider what you want to do or say!

Real story

For many years, when I was much younger, I could not care less about the impact of my words on the other side. I would speak up my mind, with absolutely no diplomacy. My focus was

> only on myself, saying what I want. I remember I was not even thinking whether my words, being too blunt quite often, would hurt the other party.
>
> I might have been a "lost case" and never managed to have a successful career, let alone a happy family life, if it weren't for my girlfriend at the time (who became some years later my wife) who, fed up with my attitude, bought me a Romanian translation of William Ury's *"Getting Past NO! – Negotiating with difficult people"*. She wrote there a special dedication for me, a dedication that I am too ashamed to show, but which served its purpose! After reading that book, I was never again the same "heartless SOB" who did not give a dime about the other side's feelings.
>
> For those of you who did not read yet Ury's book, I strongly recommend you do! Even if you are not a "walking disaster" like I was, this book will help you become better.

REASON #3
When you want to get the other side to understand better your position

In complicated situations/negotiations, one of the approaches I use to make the other side to better understand my position is to ask him/her to put himself/herself in my shoes, in other words, to view the whole situation from my vantage point.

Practically, I am asking the other side: "put yourself in my shoes. What would you do if you were me in this particular situation?" In most cases, this tactic works very well, and the other side recognizes that he/she needs to alter his/her approach as a result of a better understanding of your position.

There are, however, situations when it does not work.

Recently, I was negotiating with a senior representative of a large company and I knew I was right in my argument. I also knew that she could not agree with me, because in that way she would admit that her team made a mistake (which would have put her in a very delicate position vis-a-vis her boss, the CEO).

The funniest reply that I've ever received to my applying "put yourself in my shoes" approach was from a salesman who said: "My God, I am so happy that I am not in your shoes! I would not want this even to my worst enemies!" True, the answer was funny, but the most important thing was that it was highly effective in deflecting my tactic.

To conclude:

Always keep in mind that caring for the needs, feelings, or pain points of the other side is of paramount importance if you want to win long term deals!

6.

THE LAW OF *ALTERNATIVE*

Always go in the negotiation having at least one reliable alternative!

> *Adam chose a wife!*
> GOD

This Law is dedicated to **the alternative to the negotiation.** In other words, what the law says is that you must have another option to close your deal, should your first option fail.

I will also take the opportunity, in the second part of this chapter, to talk about **a sure-win way to counteract any of the alternatives the other party might have!** There, we will be talking about how you must **differentiate** versus your competitors, so your negotiation party will have no other option but to close the deal with you!

Let us start with the term "alternative", also known as BATNA (which is the acronym from **Best Alternative To the Negotiated Agreement,** as defined by William Ury and Roger Fisher in their book "Getting to YES!"), which in essence means **a good way out for you in case the deal goes south.**

What this Law urges you to do is quite simple:

NEVER go into a negotiation without at least one viable fallback option!

Unfortunately, as much as you prepare, there WILL be deals that will never finalize, so you will have to move forward and get your issues solved in another way. But how can you do this if you do not have an alternative? I'm sure you do not want to be in Adam's shoes, looking for a wife in Heaven...So, making sure you build another option for your needs is critical, otherwise, I can guarantee you will end up with a very poor deal, only because you failed to find an alternative.

As much as you do not believe me, it is always possible to find an alternative. Joking again, for death and taxes it is a bit more difficult to find a BATNA, but for the rest, you have a chance if you work hard enough. The keywords here are **"work hard enough"**! A strong BATNA is not given to you by God, YOU must squeeze your brains and build it. And the more you squeeze, the better BATNA you get!

Let me share with you a real situation when I successfully replaced an incumbent supplier that had lots of experience and power. This was one of my most challenging negotiations and it took almost half an year to execute and implement.

Real story

I have been working for many years with an advertising agency (let us call it "Big Ag") for one of the two critical marketing programs that I was responsible for. The second critical marketing program had been implemented by "The Other Ag",

> which was very experienced and was doing a great job too!.
>
> My company decided to look at ways to create synergies between these two critical programs, so my Purchasing colleague and I brainstormed on how we could achieve this task. Easier said than done, because each of the agencies had a lot of know-how in-house for their specific project. After several internal meetings, we decided to "bundle" the two critical marketing programs and run a tender aiming at choosing one agency for the implementation of both. Of course, we invited both the "Big Ag" and "The Other Ag" to participate in the tender, alongside other potential suppliers. This setup also created a situation in which each incumbent agency had a strength (the know-how of the program they were running in that moment) but also a weakness (the lower know-how of the program run by the other agency at the time).
>
> Both incumbent agencies presented very strong proposals, yet "The Other Agency" was overall better, so they won both programs. They had an "edge" over the "Big Ag" because they hired during the preparation period the previous GM of the "Big Ag", who brought a very strong know-how of the other program. In this way, "The Other Agency" achieved strong know-how for both marketing programs.

Having an alternative in a negotiation is a wonderful thing, trust me! It will make a big psychological difference because it will make you WANT the deal and not NEED it! You will be able to say to yourself during the negotiation: "so what if it does not go through? True, I want this deal, but I do not **need** it. I can always go back to my fallback alternative".

The psychological impact is so strong that I even heard of people that wrote their BATNA on a small piece of paper and place it in their shirt pocket, next to their heart. In this way they could be even calmer during negotiation, knowing the alternative is there.

This also reminds me of a nice joke that portrays the importance of having a relaxed mindset to perform at your best. There was one famous Rabbi called Scholl living in the USA, who asked a good friend (Zack) to lend him 10,000 USD for the weekend. Of course, Zach did it and Rabbi Scholl returned promptly the money on Monday morning. Next week, the same scenario; the following week again. After one month, Zack asked Rabbi Scholl: "Rabbi, what do you do with my money over the weekend? Do you invest it in something? Because if you do, it would be fair to share the profit with me, because I am not charging you any interest for the money". Rabi Scholl replied: "No, Zack, how could I do such a thing to you? Of course, I am not investing! But you know, each weekend I need to go to our temple and speak to those that come to pray. And believe me, a man feels much better and speaks much more inspirational when he holds 10,000 USD in his pocket"!

Doing a thorough preparation, including a market and competition assessment, you will be able to see if you can get alternatives, but also if your counterpart can get an alternative to your offer!

An excellent way to obtain a strong BATNA is to create competition for your offer (if you are a seller) or to generate options for you to purchase your needed product or service (if you are a buyer). You also need to do a proper market analysis to understand whether the market for your product or service is dominated by buyers or sellers. For now, let me give you some examples:
- If you are a **seller**, <u>always create competition for your offer by advertising your product or service</u>. For example, if you want to sell your car, you start advertising the car: with

stickers on the car's windows, on specialized car trading sites, via social networks, emails to friends, to second-hand dealers, etc. If you are selling yourself (looking for a job), you do not just sit around and wait for companies to "dream" about you! You start contacting headhunters, you register on specialized HR and recruiting sites, network with HR people, go to job fairs, use social networks like LinkedIn, etc. As soon as you have more than one request for your good or service, you start to get in good shape for a strong BATNA. Still, you must work and ensure that you get real offers from those that are interested.

- If you are a **buyer**, <u>always try to "pitch" your money and invite as many suppliers as possible to participate in the tender.</u> Make sure that you send out a truly clear brief for the requirements of the product or service you need, to get only relevant offers. Then you negotiate with each qualified supplier to end up with the best value for your money. I have organized tens of bids and trust me, if you follow the process right, you WILL get the best possible offer.

One more important point: always keep in mind that your BATNA can (and should) be improved as the negotiation unfolds. As you progress through the negotiation, you normally get additional information, either from the other party or from market intelligence. As a result, keep in mind that you need to regularly review your negotiation plan, including your BATNA to seize any opportunity for improvement.

Also, **I have one paramount advice:**

Be honest with yourself about the strength of your BATNA! Is it really strong?

If yes, then you should feel confident to walk away from a deal that is not making you happy. For example, when you are negotiating a job offer and you are not happy with what you are given, your BATNA may be simply to walk away and continue the search. This is easy if you already have a job, but if you are between jobs and your bills pile up, I am sure that you will not walk away so easily and your confidence in finding a better job will be lower.

Also, frankly speaking, from my experience, it is not easy to find a BATNA that is equally (or even better) than the current negotiation option. Obviously, if the BATNA would be better than the current negotiation, you would normally start the negotiation with the BATNA and leave the current option in the second place. So, it is especially important that you properly (and in the true cold blood) assess the current relationship and the alternative(s) to have the right perspective on your odds of success.

I am going to share now a real example that recently happened to me. It was a situation when we did not have a real, feasible alternative and we had to still close the deal, despite the difficult behavior of the other side.

Real story

We were having a 5-year long car leasing agreement for a large company fleet. Halfway through the contract we realized that we grossly overestimated the mileage of the cars at the end of the 5 years. This meant that we were paying much higher monthly fees, under the very high initial mileage assumption.

Obviously, as soon as I realized this, I asked for a meeting with the provider ("Smart Lease") and requested a recalculation of the monthly fees based on the new, more realistic mileages.

I also told Smart Lease that we would have expected them to proactively come to us with the fee reduction proposal; after all, they monitor the mileage of each car on a daily basis and they saw the trend long before I did. After a tense meeting, they reluctantly agreed to do the recalculation of the fees.

It took them almost 2 months to do the recalculation, which showed a reduction of ONE EURO per car per month, as a result of reducing the estimated mileage by 50,000 km at the end of the lease period! I could not believe my eyes! I thought they were taking us for stupid or they do not care (because we were under a valid agreement, so technically they were not forced to recalculate anything). But it was very clear to us that they were simply taking advantage of our mistake of wrongly estimating the mileage to make a hefty profit! So much about "win-win"!

I immediately started looking for alternatives and we could find two other providers that would offer us better rates than Smart Lease. Actually, we would have been better off returning all the cars to Smart Lease and pay all relevant penalties, then sign a new agreement with one of the other providers. The key issues that prevented us from selecting this option were **the cash flow impact** (paying all penalties at once would have been a significant cash out for us) and the **uncertainty whether we would be still leasing cars once the current contract would end** (we might move to buying the cars instead of leasing).

As you can see, we did not have a real, feasible alternative; we only had one on paper. So, we kept on negotiating with Smart Lease to further decrease our rates playing the card of returning the cars and paying the penalties because that would be more profitable than paying the "huge" contractual rates. After 2.5 more months (in which they charged the high rates, by the way!), they agreed to the lower fees.

Now, as promised at the beginning of this chapter, let us look at the way to counteract the other party's alternative(s): **building for your offer a very strong differentiator!**

I cannot stress enough the importance of differentiators, but I think the following quote is simply spot on and conveys the idea:

In every company, differentiation is never more important than it is in times of trouble, and that's the time when everyone tends to go to the well and equalize rather than differentiate.

JACK WELCH.
Former Chairman and CEO, *General Electric*

Differentiation is a subject discussed in marketing and branding books – not so much in negotiation literature (at least I am not aware of it). But, as mentioned earlier, this is the only sustainable way to counteract the other party's alternatives, so I decided to dedicate several pages in this book to this topic, hoping these ideas will help you win more deals.

In any negotiation, we are selling something that is of interest to the other party BUT, that is also most likely offered by our competitors!

Let me, please, explain the above. Nobody does business in a vacuum, thus for any product or service (even for your money), there is competition. So, at least one person or company offers virtually the same thing as you are. If your counterpart did his/her homework well, he/she will realize that, and you will have to show him/her why buying from you is better. Otherwise, you will not be able to sell. So, in a word, you must ***differentiate*** (positively) from your competitors.

And one of the biggest issues I have seen in negotiation (and also in marketing, by the way!) is **the lack of differentiation.** In other words, one party tries to sell something but is unable (doesn't have factual arguments) to convince his/her negotiation partner why what he/she is selling is better than the product or service offered by his/her competitors. I honestly did not believe how widespread this issue is until I saw people in my "Elite Negotiation" seminars telling me that it was the first time somebody told them about this concept and how happy they were with the results after implementing it.

For simplicity and practicality in the field of negotiation, I am going to share with you some especially useful tips and tricks to have a healthy and positive differentiation that will make the other party NEED you.

But, before anything else, let us state **the conditions for a healthy, positive differentiation**:

To differentiate, you must show to the other party:
a) one or more characteristics that set(s) your product or service apart from your competitors and
b) that those characteristics are very hard to be copied.

Let me spend a bit of time on these two concepts:
- **You must show to the other party why you are unique,** why he/she is lucky to do business with you; why it is in the other party's own interest to buy whatever you are selling. Here I underline that **you must position this in terms of the benefit for the other party**. This is valid not only when you sell goods or services, but also when you buy them (when you sell your money against those goods or services). When you "sell money", you can differentiate via many things, like

payment terms, financing facilities, the speed of cash availability, etc. Also, please note that you must be extraordinarily strong in these differentiating points!

- **Your differentiator(s) must be hard to be copied.** This means that your competitors will find it very difficult to match your differentiator. Unfortunately, many people consider that they differentiate via the "low price" they charge for their goods or service. Nothing can be further from the truth because a competitor can decrease the price to match theirs in no time. And then, where is the so-called "differentiator"?? Here I feel obliged to say that price can be, indeed a differentiator, but only a negative one! In other words, if your product is more expensive than its competitors (and no added feature can justify the price premium), then you differentiate, but in a bad way: you will not be able to sell because you are too expensive.

I can sense your question: **"OK, but practically speaking, what can I do to differentiate?"** It is not an easy task and requires strong strategic work and brand positioning. I will share in the following paragraphs 3 tips that will help you stand out if applied properly and consistently.

TIP #1
Understand what are the MUST HAVE attributes required by the consumers of the category where your product or service belongs.

Let me give you some examples: let us assume you sell a detergent. For detergents, all consumers demand that they wash/clean their clothes. A product that does not wash clothes is NOT a detergent. If you claim that your product washes clothes, then you barely say that you are a detergent – but you do not differentiate at all! Therefore, in specialized literature, these common benefits are called **Points of Parity**.

When I was Marketing Director for real, - Hypermarket I established three Points of Parity for the hypermarket category:
1. **Price** (any hypermarket must have competitive prices),
2. **Assortment** (any hypermarket must have a large, varied assortment) and
3. **Easy Shopping** (in any hypermarket it must be easy and pleasant to shop).

These points regarding hypermarket category points of parity may seem like no-brainers to you, yet you will be surprised to hear that nobody cared to make this analysis before I did it!

TIP #2
Run a diagnosis regarding the perception of your consumers vis-à-vis your Points of Parity.

When I ran this diagnosis analysis, I realized that the brand "real, -" was weak in all three Points of Parity. In other words, we were differentiating **negatively** versus our competitors. We were not the worst, but we were not the best either. That was sheer mediocracy! I do not think it could get worse than that for a brand!

So, if you are in such a situation, you must immediately design a plan to address and fix the issues on the Points of Parity. Only after the issues are resolved, you should worry about how you can positively differentiate.

TIP #3
Understand what 1-2 attributes are relevant to the target group and NOT offered (or poorly offered) by your competitors.

These are called **Points of Differentiation** and they must be your focus to close the negotiation to your advantage. But please remember to check the consumer perception vis-à-vis your desired Points of Differentiation (they must validate that those points are relevant and that your product or service indeed has them). Then understand how you can make these differentiators difficult to be copied.

Now, that we learned the steps on how to differentiate, I can hear your next question: **"All clear, but how do I create those hard-to-be-copied differentiators?"**. To properly answer this question requires a book-long presentation. Nevertheless, I will try to cover briefly in the next pages 4 ideas that will help you in a very practical way to build these points of differentiation. All have been successfully tested across the years by many large and small companies. They will serve you well!

IDEA #1
Have a proprietary technology or trade name that is only yours.

Remember Blend-a-Med (Crest) that has "Fluoristat"? Flouristat is a Trademark chemical complex developed by Procter & Gamble. And being proprietary to Procter & Gamble, nobody else can use it. Other brands use a similar approach: Adidas has ClimaCool, Jacobs Kronung has "Alintaroma", Ariel had "Carezime" etc. More recently, Fine Hygienic Holding Middle East launched the first masks, gloves, and wet wipes in the world that kill viruses and bacteria on contact because they were treated with "Livinguard", a very special, Swiss patented, substance that sterilizes the materials. Now, that is what I call a strong differentiator!

IDEA #2
Use research to prove your point

I am sure you have seen advertising for products where a statistical study is quoted to show that many consumers are satisfied with the use of the respective product or service. For example: "90% of people who used brand X were happy with the results" – and they quote a certain market study. All fine if the study is legit and independent. Watch out for the studies done "in-house" by the producers of the brand (or sellers of the service) themselves because they are by default biased – how could they say something band about their own brand or service?

Please pay close attention to the fact that **the research is statistically significant and representative**, which means the study can be extrapolated to the universe of the target group. And for this, it must be done by proper market research specialists that select a representative sample of the target group. Unfortunately, I have seen along the years many studies that were done on a handful of people that are anything but a proper sample of the target group! And imagine that the results were quoted as being generally valid and printed on the package of the product, so the consumers that are not acquainted with statistics can be fooled! Extremely unethical, so pay close attention to any fine prints and check each such claim for relevance!

IDEA #3
Leverage endorsements from celebrities, known institutes or professional associations, etc.

Did you know that the idea of using endorsers in advertising is over 250 years old? Around 1760, Josiah Wedgwood and Sons, producers of pottery and chinaware, used royal endorsements as a marketing device to show value in the company and promote to others their product ("Celebrity Endorsement – Throughout the Ages" 2004).

Other more recent examples include Michael Jordan and Nike, Roger Federer and Uniqlo or Barilla, Claudia Schiffer and L'Oréal, Neil Patrick Harris' and Heineken, Charlize Theron, and Dior, etc.

It is important to note that, to be effective, the endorser must have strong compatibility with your brand's target audience (image, perception, characteristics) and needs to be credible! Also, if a celebrity is "over-used", albeit he/she might be great, they will become significantly less effective due to the erosion of their credibility (people will believe that the celebrity would endorse virtually any brand for the right price…)

IDEA #4
Leverage the satisfaction of extremely demanding consumers that were happy with the product performance.

Remember the advertising of Ariel showing 5 stars hotel chains that use only Ariel for impeccable results? This works best for premium & super-premium brands that target above average income consumers. Also, demanding consumers or customers used in advertising must be relevant to the target group to have a strong purchase influence.

One especially important closing remark: I am sure you saw that in all those differentiation ideas **there is not a single reference to PRICE!** I feel the need to underline this because I saw it too often: brands trying to differentiate by cutting the price. Guess what: the competitor will match the next day and there is no way to go back to the old pricing unless they want to risk having a negative differentiation on price this time.

While I have tried to make a very concise presentation of the topic of differentiation, to get a truly professional and practical view on this matter, I strongly recommend that you read Jack Trout's and Steve Rivkin's excellent book **"Differentiate or Die: Survival in Our Era of Killer Competition"** (Wiley, 2008).

7.

THE LAW OF *DEADLOCK*

Never fear the deadlock, as it may be a blessing in disguise!

I know that this law, as detailed above will shock most of you, dear readers! And the reason I am saying it is because I am asking you to **consider the "frightening" deadlock as your friend, not your enemy!** I know it is counter-intuitive, but please bear with me and read on. You will understand why I am asking you to change your paradigm in this area!

Before talking about how to break it, we first need to define what "Deadlock" really is and to investigate the causes of why it occurs in so many negotiations.

A deadlock is a situation in which an agreement cannot be made; a situation in which ending a disagreement is impossible because neither side will give up something that it wants

---

A very well-known synonym to deadlock is an **impasse**. In other words, both parties hang up on their positions and do not budge.

So, why can a deadlock occur?

- While it is typical for distributive negotiations, it is important to mention that **less experienced negotiators usually enter the negotiation with a stronger tendency to be inflexible**. I have seen many times that inexperienced negotiators tend to encounter deadlocks more often than experienced negotiators.
- **Sometimes the bargaining areas of the two parties do not overlap**; the maximum acceptable of one party is lower than the minimum acceptable for the other one. In this case, as unless the two parties strive to increase "the pie", no deal can be made – and a deadlock occurs. More about this in *The Law of Expanding the Pie*.
- **In other cases, there might be a lack of trust between the parties** that makes one (or both) of them unwilling to take any risks. Trust is mandatory in a truly successful negotiation, yet there may be cases where the level of trust is low due to various reasons. Until the trust is regained, the risk of deadlock is extremely high.

Real story

One of my teammates (Karl) was recently negotiating the organization of the national sales convention. The place was a great one, a winery in the center of the country (let us call it "Best Winery"), with beautiful scenery and facilities! Everything seemed "in control" up to the moment when Best Winery requested 50% advance payment for the contract. And they were not budging!

Karl called me to present me the situation and explained that there is no other way but to agree to the advance payment. I said, "no way!" because our company does not approve any advance payments, as he was very well aware of. And I asked him to go back to Best Winery and renegotiate. He called me next day and said he managed to decrease the advance to "only" 30%. I thought I was going through the roof! The bad part was that the sales team wanted Best Winery as THE place, nothing else! So much about having any alternative...

Then it crossed my mind to ask Karl: "Tell me, WHY do they insist for the advance payment?" We are a large, multinational company, present in the market for many years, trustworthy. He could not answer. Then I asked him to call their Top Management and ask them why they do not trust us. Because it was clear for me: Best Winery did NOT trust us, otherwise they would have not asked for the advance payment!

Karl called me the following day and said he clarified the mystery: 2 years before, our company wanted to organize a large team building at the Best Winery, but cancelled 2 weeks before the event date, without paying any penalties for this last minute cancellation. As a result, Best Winery lost quite a lot of money. Now, how about that for a reason not to trust us??

I told Karl to inform Best Winery that we will sign a penalty clause for early cancellation for an amount equal to the 30% advance payment, but we will NEVER agree to the advance payment itself.

Guess what? Best Winery signed the contract. And we organized one of the best sales meetings I have ever attended!

- **The attitude of the other party may be a cause for deadlock**, if he/she becomes a bully, attacking you, or is starts being non-collaborative. Here is an example that caused me many sleepless nights...

> ### Real story
>
> I was negotiating the purchase of print media for Procter & Gamble with a very large publishing house (let us call it "Alpha Publishing"). Although at the beginning the General Manager of Alpha Publishing expressed his strong intentions to sign a new deal with us, his whole attitude during the several negotiation meetings showed inflexibility and arrogance. For your background, the print press was growing in circulation and readership year after year, hence the market was supplier dominated. We were significantly increasing our investment, but Alpha Publishing was offering us only marginal benefits (for example no additional discounts, no preferential placement of our ads in the magazines free of charge, etc.).
>
> So, as you might expect, we ended up in a deadlock and we did not sign a deal for over 6 months.
>
> We revised all our print media plans to compensate as much as possible the lack of presence in the titles belonging to Alpha Publishing. It is true, it was impossible to compensate 100%, but we obtained better conditions from the other publishing houses, so our cost per reach did not increase significantly, despite the reach being lower without the titles from Alpha. As said, we were not advertising in Alpha's for over six months and were able to re-sign an agreement only after the General Manager of Alpha was replaced. The new person was a very collaborative person, with a strong desire to obtain win-win deals.

The deadlock is feared by many negotiators, even the very experienced ones because it creates a feeling of uncertainty, of loss of control over the outcome of the negotiation. And, psychologically, we do not like to be out of control.

> **I believe that deadlock is a good thing; it can be a great opportunity to significantly improve the result of the negotiation if the situation is handled correctly.**

A deadlock normally is forcing the participants to look for other ways of reaching a mutually satisfactory agreement.

> **To break a deadlock, you must change the status quo; change the current situation that led to the deadlock.**

Unless one of the parties does a conscious effort to change the status quo, the negotiation will not get itself out of the deadlock. It is just like in the law of mechanics saying that a certain body will continue its motion unless an external force will act upon it. One more thing: there must be a mutual desire to get out of the deadlock; if only one party wants to break it and the other does not, then there is no future for the negotiation or for the relationship.

I will be sharing in the following pages **12 suggestions for actions you can take to change the status quo and release the pressure on the negotiation.** I have tried all of them across my career and each helped me a lot in times of need! The list is not at all exhaustive; please feel free to add other approaches that you tested and that work in breaking an impasse.

1. Take a break

When things heat up, one of the most effective tactics to "release the steam" is to take a break, a time-out, to postpone the discussions for later. The break can be longer or shorter, depending on how much "steam" has been accumulating. It may lead to postponing the whole meeting for later that day or even for a few days. The time gained will help each party to re-think the whole situation and see how the obstacles can be overcome.

Legend says that all diplomatic negotiations are made 90% of breaks and only 10% of talks… it says a lot about the amount of "steam" from those meetings, but also about the truth of this recommendation!

2. Postpone the "hot potato" for later and focus on agreement areas

One of the highly effective deadlock-breaking tactics is the postponement of the issue that caused the deadlock. Most negotiations include several issues to be discussed, this is why if the deadlock is caused by one of them, then try to suspend the discussions on that particular topic and move to other areas, which can be agreed easier. This tactic has two important benefits:

- It releases the "steam" built up with the issue and
- Builds areas of agreement between the parties – in this way the links between the two parties get stronger, as they have more areas of agreement than disagreement.

Later in the negotiation, when you return to the hot issue, you can show how much you advanced on the road towards the agreement, by aligning on so many areas except the "hot" one. Usually, the agreement on the issue comes easier after agreeing on other topics.

3. Changing the negotiation team or the member that caused the deadlock

Not at all seldom, a deadlock may appear due to conflicting personalities. The two teams or persons simply do not get along – on the contrary, they "hate each other's guts".

I have seen a situation like this not long ago.

Real story

An advertising agency ("Best Agency") had been working with a large client ("Betacom") for several years. In fact, Betacom was THE main client of Best Advertising, accounting for over 50% of the agency's revenue. The relationship had been historically very good until the contact person in Betacom changed. The replacement was a person that was very difficult to deal with: arrogant, tough, I might even say rude at times.

It was obvious from the first meeting that the new person in Betacom could not get along with the Account Director of Best Advertising.

The owner of Best called me to ask for my advice on how to handle the situation because it was evolving into a "smoking bomb".

Due to this relationship issue, the volume of business awarded to Best Advertising by Betacom had been steadily decreasing, so an emergency action was needed. The owner of Best Advertising proposed to get himself involved, but then, during our discussion, he realized that the root cause was the personality clash between the two people. And he could not get himself involved in each meeting. So, he decided to change the

> Account Director. The result was fast and positive – no more fights with Betacom.
>
> Side learning, the owner of Best Advertising took the learning of this scare (dropping business from his main client) as an opportunity and pitched other potential clients. As a result, he gained a large amount of new business, which compensated the loss from Betacom. And nowadays he has a healthier business, not depending so much on one single client.

4. Use humor

Another way to release the tension from the negotiation is to use humor. I like it a lot because, if done properly, it eases a lot the atmosphere. And it also makes you look human, not just a cold negotiation machine. One way I use humor is self-deprecating: I make fun of me from time to time and it worked every time.

It may be useful to memorize some famous humorous quotes and use them as appropriate. A useful resource is the book "The funniest thing you never said" by Rosemarie Jarski.

The watch out is how you use humor because it is easy to overdo it: you risk offending the other party and the result can be the opposite. Also, please pay attention to the cultural differences; the same jokes may not work in other cultures. Therefore, I always do self-deprecating humor.

Nevertheless, smiling during the negotiation is helpful, especially if it is not ironic or condescending!

5. Use arbitration/mediation of a third party

Using a third party, usually impartial to the subject can effectively de-block the impasse. If both parties aligned on who is going to be the mediator/arbitrator and that they will agree with his decision, then it is easier to reach an agreement.

The mediator can suggest ideas that are easier to be accepted by both parties because they come from an independent party. The same ideas might not be so easily accepted if they would have come from either of the parties. He can also talk in private to each party and get a better understanding of the issue versus listening to both parties at the same time. In the same way, he can propose ideas to each party separately and get feedback. Afterward, he can adjust the proposal and make it to both parties simultaneously, with confidence that it would be accepted.

6. Ask for help from the other party

This strategy is very powerful because it uses a strong psychological insight: "tingling the EGO of the other party". As said earlier, we, human beings, have EGO – we love to be the best and the smartest on the planet, if not in the whole Universe. And when somebody is asking our help, in most cases we tend to give it (our EGO is "caressed" and we are incredibly happy that we showed how smart, strong, or kind we were).

Hence, in a deadlock situation, my recommendation is to try to appeal to the other side's "mercy" or EGO.

7. Use the yin-yang principle

A quite effective strategy, it implies a shift in focus from the type of issue that caused the deadlock to another type, that you feel can be easily agreed upon. In this way, you successfully release some of the accumulated tension. And, as I said several times, the more topics you agree, the easier is to reach a final agreement because there is much more common ground than disagreement.

For example, if your deadlock is because you cannot agree on the price of an item, then propose that you put it on hold and talk about non-price items. And then you tackle these non-price items in the order of increasing difficulty (go first to the easy to agree on ones, then move gradually to more complex non-price items).

8. Recall former good relationships

Elite Negotiators™ always try to build bridges between themselves and their negotiation partners. And, a great way to do it is to find common ground – this way you reassure your partner that both of you are in for the same thing: win-win the negotiation.

By recalling the previous successful negotiations between you and the other party you encourage him to be more positive about the outcome of the current one. This is particularly effective if there was an even more difficult negotiation in the past that was finalized for mutual satisfaction.

I used this tactic several times when having internal

negotiations in the companies I was working for. Due to various reasons, colleagues of mine were more inflexible than usual, so I tried to "relax" them by recalling the long-time we worked successfully together and what a pity would be to remain in the deadlock. And it worked every time.

You may ask: "What if there is no previous relationship with the other party? What if this is the first time we meet and negotiate? How can I build on a former good relationship?" the answer is: you cannot build on the former relationship with THAT particular negotiation partner. But you can try to change this strategy a little and say that you had similar experiences with other partners (that led to a similar or even worse deadlock) and you managed to overcome the barriers. You may even suggest ways to do it by reapplying what worked in the previous situation.

9. Change the negotiation place to a neutral one

If you feel that you got in the deadlock because of the meeting place (be it your place or the office of your negotiation partner), then you can propose to halt the meeting and reconvene in a neutral place (for example a hotel conference room).

Let us be honest: negotiating on the other party's premises can be stressful, just like it is for a football team to play on the home field of the opponent. You do not know the setting very well, maybe the air conditioning is not giving the temperature that makes you feel comfortable, maybe the light is inappropriate, etc.

You gain two important things via this tactic: time, due to the break in the negotiation talks, but also a change in the environment that can release part of your stress.

10. Use the piecemeal approach (salami tactic)

There are sometimes cases of deadlocks that involve big gaps between the two positions; for example, maybe you are asking for a large discount and the other party is not willing to give it. In this case, trying to push it forward just by insisting on getting the discount will only make things worse, given the large gap.

One solution I used in some cases is a step-by-step approach (very much like the "salami" tactic). How does it work? Let us take the following example: you are estimating a yearly investment of min 100,000 Euro in advertising space in magazine A and you ask for a discount of 50% off the official rate card prices. You did your homework and your company would be the biggest advertiser in magazine A. Your bottom line is 38% and would be happy to get 45%. Magazine A representative offered a 30% discount, motivating that it is the maximum they are offering on the market. The gap between the two positions is noticeably big and the two bargaining areas do not even overlap. Not an easy situation... One way to solve the impasse is to propose a step by step approach to the discount; actually, to build and align a discount grid. In other words, you can have increasing discounts for increasing investments. You can tell the representative of Magazine A that, while you initially planned to invest the whole 100,000 Euro in their magazine, without an incentive, you can no longer guarantee the sum. So, you can propose that for an investment of up to 20,000 Euro they offer you a 30% discount. For further investments, you ask for an increased discount (the increased discount would apply to the incremental investment only). The table below simulates such a proposal:

Investment bracket	Proposed discount	Weighted discount for maximum bracket investment*
0 – 20,000 Euro	30%	30.0%
20.001 – 30,000 Euro	35%	31.7%
30.001 – 50,000 Euro	40%	34.0%
50,001 – 70,000 Euro	45%	37.9%
70,001 – 100,000 Euro	50%	41.5%

* For example, if you only invest 20,000 Euro you get a 30% discount. If you invest 30,000 Euro, you get a 30% discount for the first 20,000 Euro and 35% for the following investment up to 30,000 Euro (which means you get a 35% discount for the 10,000 Euro additional). The same reasoning applies for the following brackets as well.

In the end, you can obtain a 41.5% average discount for the 100,000 Euro investment, which is above your minimum acceptable and it gives you flexibility in terms of investment. With an investment of only 70,000 Euro (versus your total 100,000 Euro), you get practically a 38% average discount (your minimum acceptable).

11. Reinforce how much was previously agreed

One of the most powerful strategies in negotiation is the investment strategy. Make the other party invest resources (usually time and/or energy) in the negotiation and it will be much easier to get to an agreement.

Therefore, I always recommend sequencing the issues in the **increasing order of complexity**. In this way, you have extremely high chances to get to align many topics until you reach a deadlock situation. And, when it occurs, then simply say: "Look how much we have achieved so far. We both made a lot of effort and are close to finalizing this negotiation. It would be a pity to kill it all now..." You will see how powerful and amazingly effective this tactic is.

12. Look again at the issue, but from a different perspective

It is a natural tendency of humans that, when we concentrate long on an issue or problem, we tend to get stuck on one approach and do not see other possibilities. This is known as "thinking inside the box" because we only think within the known boundaries. It is very frequently encountered because we like the comfort of established routes. After all, they are safe and do not require a lot of energy from us (remember the principle of physics that says that "all systems tend to go by themselves to a state of lowest energy and highest entropy"? – same applies to humans – we love to be lazy...)

"Looking outside the box" is the opposite: try to evaluate the situation from a completely different perspective, with different eyes. Easier said than done because we are biased: we have been looking at the problem from one angle for so long that we believe there is not possible another angle. So, how do we achieve this looking from a different angle? There are several approaches:

- Try to explain the situation or issue to someone who did not have anything to do with it. Explaining will help you clear your mind and understand even the smallest details, but it can also benefit you from the advice of the person whom you explained.

- Ask your negotiation counterpart to put himself in your shoes. What would he do if he were you in the same situation? The benefit of this approach is larger than you might expect. It proved to me in many cases that the other party is prone to drop part of his demands after being put in such a situation.
- Put yourself in the shoes of the other party and see if things look different from their vantage point. Perhaps they are right, and you do not see the full picture!
- Take a time-out, go back to the office, and put the problem aside. Re-evaluate it later in the day or even after 1-2 days if the negotiation schedule allows it. In the meantime, force yourself not to think of the problem.

I hope you could see by now that there is no need to be afraid of a deadlock! While nobody likes it, if managed properly, it can be a real help in achieving even better results versus the situation before the deadlock! Just remember to suppress your EGO and brainstorm ways to progress the negotiation despite the uncomfortable situation of the deadlock.

8.

THE LAW OF *TOTAL VALUE*

Always look at the Total Negotiation Value, not solely at the price paid!

I particularly consider this Law truly relevant these days because of the increasingly obsessive focus on price in most of the negotiations, to the detriment of other variables, that sometimes prove to be even more important.

From my personal experience, the ONLY way to achieve a sustainable result in a business negotiation that is not a "one-time" event is to focus on the VALUE that each party obtains out of the deal. And by VALUE, I mean the ratio of what we get for what we pay:

$$Perceived\ Value = \frac{What\ we\ get}{What\ we\ pay}$$

Beware of the especially important expression **"Perceived Value"**! This means that we are talking about PERCEPTION, which, by definition, is SUBJECTIVE! For one person, the deal can be of great value (because he/she feels he/she is getting a lot out of it), while for another person the same deal can be a poor one (because what he/she pays doesn't justify the benefit).

All of us have heard this expression (and sometimes even felt it ourselves) that something "It's not worth the money". We also sometimes felt that something was so important that we would pay "no matter how much" to get it. In both cases, the same equation is involved.

I made this prologue to this important Law because we must be aware of the fact that, unless we understand what is important for the other side, it will be extremely difficult to close a genuinely good deal. And, as you can see, the (in) famous PRICE is only one part of the equation. I remember someone telling me that if he does not like a specific brand of clothes, he would never take a single item, even if the item would be for free!

Before we dive into the details of each of the two pillars of the Value equation, I want to stress one paramount point: **it is critical that you are certain about the reliability of the other party!** This means you must do your background checks and due diligence with the utmost care (as explained in *The Law of Preparation*, earlier in this book) and be as sure as possible about their willingness and capability to sustain the implementation of the deal that you two are negotiating! This includes the ability to deliver the **quality** you requested, but also their **financial health**, as you need a supplier for the longer term.

Now let us go back to the value equation and analyze the two items one by one:

"WHAT WE GET"

There are three main categories of things we get in negotiation: the actual business needs that we want to be satisfied, the long term (or not) relationship with the other party, and the total value (commercial, financial, and operational) obtained in the negotiation.

Let us take these one by one:

1. The business needs that should be satisfied with what we get (BN).

For example, if we are buying spare parts for industrial equipment, how well are the purchased spare parts answering the specific engineering needs of the factory? Is the product that is offered fulfilling all technical specs? Here please pay attention to have all the specs fulfilled but be attentive not to get a piece of equipment that offers MORE than what you need. To make a quite simple comparison, if you need a Volkswagen Passat, be attentive not to be sold a Rolls Royce if you do not need one! I have seen situations when the supplier was explaining all the benefits of the "Rolls Royce", but we did not need 50% of those extraordinary additional benefits!

It is worth looking at all characteristics of the more expensive products in comparison with the cheaper ones: what does the more expensive product have as <u>additional features</u> and the cheaper one does not? Are these additional features relevant to you? Can they help you drive lower Total Cost of Ownership? Or drive a lower cost per use? Or help the product last longer than its competitors (recall the famous ads for Duracell?) Or help improve the satisfaction of your consumers?

If the specs of the goods you want to buy are OK, how about the other aspects: servicing, warranty, spare parts supply, the lifetime of the device, etc.?

Beware of the specs that are **promised** in the tender and the ones that are **delivered** after the company won the deal! I lived myself through several cases like this, one of the most unpleasant ones happened when I was working in METRO.

> ### Real story
>
> My Marketing Department was responsible for Private Labels as well: we planned to launch a range of cornflakes under our private label and we organized a tender with several potential suppliers. All accepted to participate in the tender, sent samples and quoted. We selected one that we believed offered the best value: very good taste and very good price. We should have been more careful! A couple of months later we started getting consumer complaints from shoppers as well as from company employees that our corn flakes had a rancid taste. We could not believe it, yet we went to get samples from stores, from various production batches. And all had the same awful smell and taste!
>
> Investigating the root cause, we concluded that the supplier tried to cut corners and used poorer quality raw materials to keep his manufacturing costs low.

2. The long-term relationship you wish with the other party (LTREL).

Is this going to be "the beginning of a beautiful friendship" as they said at the end of Casablanca movie? Many times, a mutually beneficial and long-term relationship will pay huge dividends because the parties will go beyond the regular duty calls and help each other in times of need! And trust me, sometimes these extra helping hands in times of big need are priceless. So, consider very seriously the relationship when looking at the value equation!

3. The financial advantages obtained during the negotiation

Some of the most important ones relate to the cost savings, cost avoidances, one-time financial benefits, and the improvements in the working capital:

The deal cost savings (CS)

These refer to any cost reductions you make when purchasing a good or service. Different companies have different methodologies for reporting these, so I will not go into technicalities here. But, as a matter of principle, a cost-saving (cost reduction) must have a positive impact on the business' bottom line (or, in other words, increase the profitability of the business).

The deal cost avoidances (CA)

These refer to avoiding a future cost increase that will not result in a reduction of the price that you pay. While you cannot see this impacting DIRECTLY the bottom line (the profitability), the fact that you AVOIDED a price increase means that you helped avoid an additional cost which would have lowered the profitability. Let me give you some examples (without being exhaustive):
- Negotiating not to pay the inflation (in other words, while you normally would pay a higher price due to inflation, you negotiate that this is absorbed by the seller, either 100% or

partially)
- Obtaining free/additional products. As an example, you may get one free product for 3 products purchased. This means that the price of the fourth product is cost avoidance.
- Negotiating the exit from a contract in more favorable terms vs what is specified in the contract. For example, you may have a penalty clause in the contract in the case of early termination. If you negotiate that this is reduced (or canceled), this represents avoiding a cost.

The one-time financial benefits of the deal (OTFB)

Sometimes you do not get a cost-saving/reduction in the negotiation, yet you get some one-off financial benefits like <u>one-time</u> cost benefits, discounts, rebates, signing bonuses, etc. These are non-sustainable, in other words, you will not get them recurring for the lifetime of the deal. As an example, let us assume you are negotiating to buy cleaning products to be used in your hotel. The total spend is 150,000 Euro and the supplier might offer you a 1% signing bonus because this would be the first year of your collaboration (1% of 150,000 Euro means 1,500 Euro that is a one-time financial benefit). But this is to be paid only in the first year, therefore it is a "non-sustainable" cost advantage.

The improved payment terms (a.k.a. the working capital benefits) (WCB)

These refer to improving the cash flow of your business by either:
- increasing the number of days at which you pay your debts (=increasing the length of your short-term liabilities, which allows you to keep your cash in your pockets for longer), or
- by reducing the inventory levels that you hold (which means

releasing some of the money that is tied up in the stocks).

Please note that it is extremely important to assess whether extending the payment terms with a supplier makes financial sense. In other words, what do you give up in return for the extended payment terms? In finance they look at the "cost of capital" and they compare the interest rate the company would have to pay to the bank to finance those days of payment vs the financial benefit obtained from the supplier in return for giving up the payment terms.

For example, if you want to increase your payment terms from 30 days to 90 days of a 100,000 Euro invoice and the supplier wants 1% financing cost upcharge to the cost for that (1% of 100,000 Euro = 1,000 Euro), this is equivalent to paying 1% interest rate to a bank to get a 60 days loan worth of 100,000 Euro. You need to compare this 1% interest rate for the 2 months extension (equivalent to circa 6% per annum) with the interest rates requested by banks in the market. If the banks charge less than that, then it is NOT worth paying 1% to extend the payment terms.

"WHAT WE PAY"

Here we look at all monetary ways of paying the benefits of the negotiation. And while the actual absolute purchase price is obviously the most important one, there are other things to consider beyond it, like the total cost of ownership, the potential hidden costs, and the actual cost per use:

1. The absolute purchase price (APP)

I think this is straightforward: it refers to the actual buying price of the good or of the service. While I do not want to spend a lot of time on this trivial topic, I urge you to look, when doing a tender, at the price of each participant and at what they offer for that price. What is included and what is not? Do you need all the features that you are offered? In a recent tender at our brewery, we were buying a conveyor and one of the suppliers made us an offer that was double vs the lowest one. Most of the difference was due to some extra features that we did not need.

By the way, if you get a price that looks too good to be true, then I bet it IS too good to be true (see the Lowballing tactic in the Tactics chapter of "The Elite Negotiator™" for more details!). So, remember, never assume, and always ask what is included and what is not included in the price!

2. The Total Cost of Ownership (TCO)

In the case of some equipment, there is more than the buying price that you must think of; you must consider as well **the maintenance and repair costs of the equipment not covered by the warranty for the whole period you intend to use it.**

As the acquisition price is usually significantly higher than the maintenance costs, we tend to neglect the later, but this is wrong! It is well known that most of the companies in the auto industry (and not only) make their profits from servicing the cars they produce. Also, you should do your due diligence and investigate the product reliability beyond the warranty, to assess what would be the Total Cost of Ownership for the lifetime of the product you are buying.

Beware of going for the "cheapest" offer without having a reality check for the features that are offered!

3. The potential hidden costs (PHC)

I will give you another real example:

> **Real story**
> I have heard of a hotel that was buying slightly cheaper toilet paper, aiming at making savings. Nothing wrong with that approach!
>
> They had an alternative that was approx. 7% more expensive due to a special technology embedded that allowed the paper to dissolve in water very fast, much faster than its competitors. But they went for the cheapest option, not believing that the extra feature is worth the extra 7% in the purchase price.
>
> Later in the year, the hotel had a serious incident with the central sewage getting clogged and they had to close the hotel for 2 days to fix it. What was the total business impact due to repairs and the loss of business? 34,500 Euro!! In only 2 days!!

Was it worth going for the cheapest product and making an apparent "saving" in the first place? I let you decide!

4. The actual cost per use (ACPU)

We sometimes feel incredibly happy and fortunate when we buy something at a good deal (=low purchase price). But, if we talk about a product that is used multiple times, we must also look, besides the overall purchase price at the actual cost per use. This means the cost per each use of the product.

Let us see some real examples:

Real story

Buying something as trivial as kitchen paper roll towels can be tricky too, because you need to be careful when assessing the technical specs: what is the length of the total roll, what is the length of the individual sheet of paper, how many sheets do they have in a roll, how many sheets are needed during a normal use etc.

You may end up buying cheaper rolls, but the quantity per use may be higher, therefore the cost per use can be higher vs other, more expensive (per piece) products.

A friend told me about his company selling kitchen paper rolls having 150 sheets per roll. A competitor was selling very similar paper rolls, claiming to have exactly the same 150 sheets per roll, but in reality, there were only 146 sheets. Not a significant difference after all, right? Not so! Considering the total value of the deal he was trying to get, these 4 sheets less for his competitor meant approx. 250,000 Euro lower cost for his "cheating" competitor!

> ### Real story
>
> In the brewery, we are using shrink film to wrap the pallets with finished beer. And the custom is that the film is bought by weight (the suppliers sells rolls of shrink film by kilogram).
>
> But the film is wrapped on a central core made of carton and guess what: the carton core has its weight too! So, when you buy the film roll (and consider the total package weight, which includes not only the film but also the carton core), you buy the core at the price of the film too! How about that for the price of simple carton??
>
> I have seen situations of significant weight difference between rolls of various producers due to different core weights, not because there was more film on the film roll of one producer vs the film roll of another.
>
> As a result, after understanding how much money we lost by not paying attention to this apparently trivial aspect, we have changed the approach and we are currently buying the shrink film NET of the core – and, as a result, we get a hefty saving!

Or, in another case, also with paper rolls, the more expensive product (by 20% vs its immediate competitor), lasted 50% longer in normal use!

Then, I am asking you: which product is worth buying from a cost-efficiency point of view? **The cheaper one per piece or the cheapest one per use?**

As you could see, there are MANY aspects to consider besides the actual purchase price when thinking about the Total Negotiation VALUE. We must never underestimate any of these elements, as they can improve (or decrease) the total negotiation value.

Therefore, now the value equation becomes a bit more complex (I am using the abbreviations mentioned above besides each term):

$$Perceived\ Value = \frac{BN \times LTREL \times CS \times CA \times OTFB \times WCB}{APP \times TCO \times PHC \times ACPU}$$

And by now, I'm sure you see that in many cases the actual purchase PRICE (APP) may be of much lower importance versus the other aspects mentioned above, especially the quality of the good or service delivered or the sustainability of the delivery. I still recall my Vice-President of Procurement Europe telling me:

> "Procurement's first and most important mandate is to ensure the supply of the goods or services that are critical to the business. All other financial benefits like the cost savings, cost avoidances, etc. while important, are of secondary importance when compared to the supply assurance!"

9.

THE LAW OF *EXPANDING THE PIE*

Always look at ways to expand the subject of negotiation and deliver value over the long term!

Negotiations over a shrinking pie are especially difficult because they require an allocation of losses. People tend to be much more easygoing when they bargain over an expanding pie.

DANIEL KAHNEMAN
Israeli American psychologist and economist

A strong relationship goes beyond any one deal!

JOHN E. PEPPER JR.
Former CEO, President, and Chairman of the Board, *Procter & Gamble Co.*

You remember that in the *Law of Preparation* we looked at the two fundamental interests in any negotiation: the interest for the **material gain** and the interest in the **relationship**. And we said that these two are in an inverse proportionality, in other words, the more we want one, the less we get from the second.

Depending on the focus we have in the negotiation we have two main types of negotiations:
- the **positional negotiation** (also known as **distributive negotiation, negotiation over a FIXED pie** or **win-lose**) that is focused almost exclusively on the material gain, and

- the **integrative negotiation** (also called **negotiation over an EXPANDING pie**, or **win-win**) that is focused on both the material gain AND the relationship. In this type of negotiation, both parties try to "expand the pie" such that each gets more than initially thought. This is the highly recommended approach for business negotiations.

This Law is focused on sharing with you some strategies that I have personally tested over the years and that will help you achieve many more win-win negotiations.

However, before we dive into these strategies, I would like to make an important comment that summarizes the essence of the approach:

> **WIN-WIN means that both parties obtained a satisfactory agreement (one that falls satisfactory within the boundaries they put for the negotiation)**

I heard some years ago a joke, in which somebody explained his understanding of the win-win in negotiation: "Win-win means that I win twice!"

Joke aside, it does not mean that, if the two parties finally signed a deal (good or bad) it is win-win. Trust me, if the deal is not comfortable to you vis-à-vis your limits, it will not live through to implementation because your needs will not be satisfied. The same is true for the other party. Imagine you are looking for a job and the job market is exceptionally soft; you get one offer, but it is significantly worse than your current job. So, what do you do? If your current job is "hell" for you and you cannot live there anymore, then you will, for sure, take that offer. But be honest: won't you continue looking for another, better job? Of course, yes! The same happens with the deals; if it is a genuinely good deal (both parties win), then it will be a solid deal. If not, then one party will soon "defect" and look for another deal partner.

I have recently asked John E. Pepper Jr, the former CEO, President and Chairman of Procter & Gamble what he feels are the key ingredients for a successful deal, for a truly win-win one.

> "I believe there are two key things that are of paramount importance for a real win-win deal. The first one is **trust**. Without trust there is nothing; trust is the foundation of every relationship. The second one is a **genuine understanding of the other party's needs**.
>
> The formation of the P&G-Walmart team is a great example of that. Tom Muccio, who was running P&G's US Food business came to me when I was President and proposed that we form a multifunctional team of over 40 P&G people that would be located at Walmart's HQ. The team's role was to disproportionately drive the growth of the joint P&G-Walmart business in a way that has never been done before.
>
> If it were not for my deep trust in Tom, I probably would have never agreed to this "experiment". But I trusted him, and I knew he truly understood both our needs as well as Walmart's. So, I along with the rest of the Top Management, went for it. And the rest is history! Thousands of other producers did similar multifunctional teams with Walmart and with other large retailers. The producer-retailer relationships have never been the same since then, going to a new level of mutual development.
>
> And it all happened because a trustworthy person knew deeply the needs of each party and had the guts to make it happen!"

And now, after we clarified the basics, let us start the discussion of the **8 strategies to achieve a real WIN-WIN** that I distilled for you from my business negotiation experience.

1. Make sure you really want a win-win relationship with the other party.

You may think I am crazy to state this. But I am not (or at least people around me tell me I am not (yet) crazy…). Most people make a big mistake when deciding on the desired relationship: "win-win' (integrative) versus "win-lose" (distributive) because they focus mostly on their winning and, sometimes, trying to give something to the other party. They claim "win-win", but in fact, they are going for "Win!". What is the difference? In the "win-win", both parties try hard to get to a sustainable long-term agreement, in which truly **both** will win. In the "Win!" approach, one party is concerned about winning and it does not really care what happens to the other party. The other party may win, may partially win, or may even lose. This is a false "win-win" and you should be very careful when deciding what you want in terms of the relationship. If you genuinely want the both-win one, then get involved and work for it!

2. Focus on understanding what the real needs of the other party are.

I am returning to the *Law of Shoes,* specifically to the "Iceberg theory" because it is of paramount importance in effective negotiation. Remember what I told you: nobody (and I mean "**nobody**") will tell you openly what his real motivators are. Would you tell the other party that your boss will fire you if you do not sign this contract? Or that you will get a promotion if you sign? Of course not, because you fear that the other party will take advantage of it. So, you, as an "Elite Negotiator™", must consider it as your top priority finding out the drivers of the other party: why is really the other side negotiating with you?

But how do you get this information? Obviously, you do not simply ask the other guy: "Why are you negotiating with me?" You need to collect as much information as possible about the other party, then you need to check your assumptions in the negotiation meeting. Subtly, of course, using dialogue and especially open-ended questions. During this questioning process, keep your ears open and listen carefully. Studies are showing that the experimented negotiators will use questions twice as much as the novice negotiators and will listen twice as much as well.

3. Never keep the negotiation one-dimensional

The recipe for failure in a win-win negotiation is the use of the one-dimensional approach. What is this? It is quite simple: if you have only one issue to discuss with the other party, then you are in a one-dimension negotiation. The classical examples are the open market bargaining over fruits or vegetables: you want 10 kg of potatoes and you are negotiating with the farmer the price. Truth be told, even this one can be made multi-dimensional, but, for the sake of demonstration, let us assume you are bargaining over the price only. In one-dimension, what constructive options do you have? Not many, because there is a "give and take" approach and the more one side gets, the less is left for the other side. And this is the true distributive negotiation: negotiation over a "fixed pie".

Hence, always be flexible and think of other elements that

can be negotiated. For example, if the price is the key dimension, you can add non-price related elements in the negotiation as well. I mention below some dimensions you can add (there are many more, so really brainstorm for all relevant ones in your situation):

- **Payment terms:** do you pay on delivery or later? After how many days? – Here you have a negotiation margin.
- **Delivery conditions:** do you deliver to their location or they come and pick up the goods? Do you deliver all at once or in batches?
- **Warranty:** length of the warranty, conditions for an extended warranty, cost-sharing of the extended warranty, etc.
- **Multiple purchases:** how would the negotiation shape out if you want to purchase more items or a larger quantity?
- **Return rights:** can you return the unused merchandise? If yes, under what conditions?

You can see that there are other elements you can bring in the negotiation, such that, if you cannot get the desired price, at least you get a strong advantage in another area. For example, if you can't get the price, maybe you get more advantageous payment terms (ex 90 days versus standard 45 days) or you might get free delivery (which in some cases, might offset the price difference).

4. During the negotiation, explore intensively the common ground with the other party

I have seen across the years in my negotiations that experienced ("Elite") negotiators emphasize and stress the common ground (common elements) they have with the other party over three times as much as inexperienced negotiators. Why is this important? The focus on common elements is very powerful in strengthening the trust with the other party. It shows that you and your counterpart are bound together by common interests and that the result of the negotiation will positively affect both of you. It also shows that you both must lose if the deal falls.

As already mentioned, this strategy is also particularly good in deadlock situations when both parties feel that the whole "thing" is blocked and there is no way to go forward. By taking a pause, thinking about all the progress made so far and how many interests you have in common with the other party, you have high chances to release the pressure and unlock the deal.

I also think this strategy makes wonders in the tough negotiations with people that have the same interest as you have, but, due to various reasons (for example EGO), play as opposing party. The best example is the negotiation between retailers and producers, where both parties have the same interest (selling as much as possible), but they play as like they are on totally opposing sides (EGO driven behavior...). You can read more about retailer – producer negotiations in the dedicated chapter of my book "The Elite Negotiator™".

5. Always look for multiple solutions to each of the issues under negotiation and any possible trade-offs

The Elite Negotiators always know that by brainstorming for several solutions for each of the issues under discussion will ultimately lead to a win-win solution. And they do it two times more frequently than average, inexperienced negotiators. Why is that? Because by having several options for each issue, it will be easier for the other party to relate to at least one solution. On the contrary, if you give only one option for each issue, imagine what will be the odds that the other party will find exactly that option as the ideal solution for him.

Also, imagine what potential trade-offs could move the deal forwards; what can you exchange in return for something that is of higher value to you?

Let us assume you know that **longer contract term** is of high interest for the other side. In this case, think what is of high importance to you and you could ask from the other side, in return for signing this longer deal (for example, you may ask for an additional price advantage, or additional delivery advantage, or improved payments terms, etc.)

6. Take time to think and analyze the negotiation process as it unfolds

An experienced negotiator will listen more than will talk and will take the time to truly understand the meaning of what the other party said (we will discuss this in the *Law of Outstanding Communication*). Thus, he will make fewer counterproposals per hour for each issue (from my own observations, roughly two times less than the inexperienced negotiator).

This strategy is good because it also employs the "acceptance time" or "consideration time" concept: people need time to "digest" any information and it is also a sign of respect and consideration for the other party to (or at least pretend to) think about the offer.

I have used the "acceptance time" many times in my negotiations and it helped me a lot. Therefore, I always have my laptop and my calculator (or, the phone with the calculator app) with me in all negotiations. Besides giving the other side the impression that I seriously consider his/her proposal, I also do the actual computations to make sure I don't make any mistakes.

Needless to say, if you take the time to think, you might even get a good idea of how to move forward!

7. Build trust with the other party

Trust is so important in a win-win relationship approach that I cannot stress it enough. I would even say that trust is mandatory in many aspects of life! Just think about the first question you ask yourself before investing your savings in a bank: is the bank trustworthy? The same with relationships. **Trust is paramount; it is the foundation of everything else.** The lack of trust will ruin any relationship!

Building trust is not at all an easy process – I sometimes compare it with savings in a bank. You need first to deposit money in the bank to have what to withdraw. The same is with trust: first, you need to show and prove that you are trustworthy, then you will benefit from this image.

But how do you build trust? I strongly recommend you use a binary, "fool-proof" recipe, that works 100% of the time:

1. **Keep all your commitments!** ALWAYS! There is nothing worse than somebody you cannot rely on.
2. **Do it consistently and for the long term.** In this way, you will "save" a capital of image and trust that will allow you in the future to "withdraw" in case of need (for example if you don't keep your commitment once after having a strong history of keeping it, the other will "forgive" you easier than somebody who is at the beginning and has no history)

I will give you a true (and also sad) example to show you the importance of trust and what happens when you do not respect some basic rules when doing business.

> ### Real story
>
> I was approached by the CEO of an important agency that was active in several countries outside Romania to help him prepare for a very important business pitch that involved 8 markets, including 3 countries where he was not doing business in. He needed my help to coordinate the preparations for this pitch across all 8 countries and help in getting local partners in those 3 countries where he was not present.
>
> One important element: I knew this agency CEO since 1996 and we did many projects together while I was in Procter & Gamble. I never had any reasons to doubt his honesty and character. On the contrary, he managed some really "miraculous" project implementations when the time was running out. He always kept his word and delivered what he promised. And not only for one year, but for almost 15 years of collaboration.
>
> So, I had no reason to doubt his character. The time was very short, and he came down to Bucharest to talk about how we will prepare for the pitch. I strongly recommended him to possible partners in 2 of the 3 countries where he was not operating. I took over myself the preparation for the third one. Here is when I made my big mistake: **we did not put anything formally in writing (at least a draft MoA or Non-Disclosure Agreement) as far as the collaboration between his agency and the ones I recommended was concerned.**
>
> We only relied on some exchanged emails on the subject and worked like hell to finish all preparations in due time. We finished everything and submitted the materials in due time.
>
> Then, the shock came: he took all our work and gave it to some

> other agency he was friends with, to submit it in the pitch, without mentioning anything about the agencies that worked on those materials. Needless to say, the CEO refused to answer any of our emails or phone calls, aimed at clarifying the situation. He did not reply to the notification done by the lawyer hired by the two cheated agencies. As we did not have any formal agreement, the matter could never be settled in court…

Incredibly sad story… it still hurts me, but I learned my lesson: as my dear friend John E. Pepper loves to say, **"trust people, but do it with your eyes open!"**

8. Keep a positive attitude and try to diffuse conflicts at the very early stage.

Never take it at a personal level and "Tame the lion" from the other side. The Elite Negotiator™ will do his best to avoid personal attacks towards the other party, as well as the use of irritating comments that raise the nervousness level of the other party (on average, the experienced negotiator uses five times fewer irritators than the inexperienced negotiator). In this way, the Elite Negotiator™ will help building stronger relationships.

It is also true that in some cases **the other party may be the one creating the irritators and the conflicts**, so you are not in control. Then your only option is to decide whether you want to "play the conflict game" or use "a relationship fire extinguisher". If you want to finalize the deal (in a win-win manner) then I strongly recommend the **"relationship fire extinguisher" strategy**.

I have used this strategy many times and it never failed. It was particularly important in internal negotiations, especially those I had with my Purchasing colleagues from retail. Many of the buyers tend to behave internally in a similar way they do with their suppliers: tough, many times arrogant, inflexible; with the attitude "it's my way or the highway". At first, it shocked me to see that they have the same approach internally, but then I realized that this is the way they were taught to behave, and they simply don't care about the relationship with the other party. Two of the worst only knew the "shouting" strategy; they would not even let you finish your sentence and they would jump to the wrong conclusion and get angry. It was truly pathological... So, given that I had to work with them on many projects, I had the choice to either get into a fight with them and start shouting as well, or try to "tame" them. My choice was always the more difficult one: to "tame" versus having "a mud bath"! So, each time they would start bursting in angriness, I would start smiling back, let them finish their "steam outburst" and then I would tell them: "I don't understand why we waste so much energy in this internal fighting. Aren't we on the same side? Don't we want the same: increased sales for the company? Then why don't we spend the same energy on finding better ways to gain a business advantage?" I would be speaking with a smile on my face all the time. In most cases, they would calm down and get more reasonable. A couple of times, they were "extra steamy" and I proposed that we meet a bit later over a coffee and start over again. And then it worked.

When faced with a "lion", especially an angry one, always keep in mind the following: any war needs two belligerent parties. If only one wants the war, but the other does not join in, no war can take place.

As you could see, there are many ways to achieve a win-win outcome for your negotiation, if you and the other party want it!

If you feel that only you want the win-win and the other side doesn't, I recommend you show them the advantages of this approach for them (show "what's in it for THEM!", in other words, their gain longer-term).

10.

THE LAW OF
OUTSTANDING COMMUNICATION

Always make a priority to listen disproportionately more than to speak!

> *There is only one rule for being a good talker – learn to listen.*
> CHRISTOPHER MORLEY
> American journalist

> *People live too much of their lives on email or the Internet or text messages these days. We're losing all of our communication skills.*
> TRACY MORGAN
> American comedian

This Immutable Law is dedicated to the way we communicate in a negotiation. Or better said, the way we communicate in life! Let me say it straight from the beginning: we all have room for improvement as far as our communication ability is concerned!

To be a successful, "Elite Negotiator™", you MUST have an outstanding communication ability

---

An Elite Negotiator™ can listen effectively, understand the

real meaning of what is being said (not only the obvious words but also the subtleties behind them) and speak as well effectively, such that he maximizes the outcome of the negotiation while maintaining a positive relationship.

I know what you are thinking right now: communication is a very tricky subject... We all believe that we are great communicators; in most cases, this can be translated as "I am a good communicator because I can speak as much as I want, and nobody gets upset". Unfortunately, this is not true...

But what is "effective communication"?

G. B. Shaw gave a rather pessimistic perspective in his reflection: **"The single biggest problem in communication is the illusion that it has taken place"**.

Anatole France had a better perspective when he said that **"The more you talk, the fewer people will remember from your speech"**. This means that an effective communicator should be balanced as far as the amount of talking is concerned.

Kelly Fordyce touched a sensitive point: many times, we speak more than we should, to show that we are the smartest in the room... **"Language is a wonderful thing. It can be used to express thoughts, to conceal thoughts, but more often, to replace thinking."**

In my point of view,

"effective communication" means the effective exchange of information between the parties engaged in the communication process, leading to a mutually satisfactory result.

It includes actions like active listening, asking questions, clarification of what has been said, summarizing.

In the following pages, I will take you through **a detailed list that summarizes the top communication traits of Elite Negotiators™**.

1. Asking questions

It is not surprising that successful, Elite Negotiators™ ask questions twice as much as inexperienced negotiators. In this way, they make sure they gather information about the interests of the other side, they test assumptions, explore possible options to move the negotiation forward, and build and strengthen the relationship with the other side.

2. Clarifying

The second important trait relates to making sure what you understood was indeed intended to be like that. When you want to clarify something, use words like "precisely" or "exactly". For example: "More precisely, what did you mean by…"; "What exactly did you mean by…."

In my point of view, there is nothing like "too much clarification". Of course, if you clarify each sentence of the other party, you may be asked to check your sanity and IQ but, you must use it reasonably to avoid bigger headaches later.

Now let me share with you a real example that frustrated me greatly at the time.

> **Real story**
>
> I remember the situation when I was negotiating the implementation of a very important and strategic marketing program for Procter & Gamble with a foreign agency.
>
> The CEO of the company and the International Business Director were present at the meeting. I was accompanied by the Brand Manager of the brand that benefited from the program.
>
> One very important information to you, the reader: at the time, the CEO was not speaking English very well, therefore, many times he was addressing us in his native language, asking the business director to translate. As a result, the talks were very lengthy and required us to spend a lot of energy in the meeting.
>
> Because of this language barrier, many times we had to ask for clarification and, to our surprise, after asking for the clarification, we got another message, different from the initial one. While it was never any suspicion of bad intent from the agency side, quite frequently we felt like dancing: one step forward, two steps backward. As a result, the negotiation took about 3 months until we found a mutually satisfactory way.

What's the learning of the story? Do not be shy and ask for clarification. Better to look stupid than to BE stupid because you misunderstood some elements.

3. Checking for understanding

Never assume that your message got across to the other side exactly as you intended to be!! I fell into this trap many times; I thought my message was truly clear and I did not check if the understanding of the other part is the one I intended. And, to my surprise, it was not!

So, always do regular checks for understanding during a negotiation meeting. Just pause the discussion at some point (ideally before or after a break) and say: "Let's just recap the key points discussed and agreements reached so far". And you start doing it. You will see that in some cases you will get feedback from the other part about some points that were not clear.

Also, after the other party states a certain point or demand, make sure you paraphrase and recap what was said. Say: "Let me, please, recap what you just said, to make sure I understood correctly". And you start doing it immediately. This approach has two important benefits: it makes you feel 100% sure about what was said and, at the same time, buys you time to think.

4. Active listening

Yes, I know: we all listen; we all listen very well. So, why do we keep on discussing this? Because we do not listen well! The fact that we "hear" what's been said doesn't mean that we "listen"!!! It is a big difference between "hearing" and "listening"! Before going forward, please take a minute and think about the differences. It is more difficult than you initially thought, right? Of course, it is! We are so accustomed that "listening" and "hearing" are almost synonymous than we fail to differentiate between them. Actually, "hearing" is just the physical, mechanical process of sounds reaching our ears and being transformed into music, words noise, etc. "Listening" is the psychological process of **understanding** the meaning of the words, music, noise, etc. So, when we say: "I'm listening to you", we are implying that we also **understand** what is being transmitted.

The Elite Negotiators™ use skillfully the active listening; as a matter of fact, they do it twice as much as novice negotiators.

Everything sounds simple, right? In theory yes, in practice no… There is an old saying of Evelyn Waugh: **"Americans don't listen so much as they wait for their turn to speak"**. I wonder whether that is only valid for Americans, or does it apply to all of us?? So, the unanimous conclusion is that "listening is difficult". But why is it? Good question! I gathered here some potential answers, but for sure this list is not at all exhaustive. Feel free to add to it your own reasons:

- Historically we have been "programmed" to believe that those who talk more are rewarded (you look better in front of your boss if you have a higher "share of voice" in meetings); it is a sign of "assertiveness" and "leadership". Hence, we find it difficult to listen to… I completely disagree; it is not the **quantity** of talk but the **quality** of talk that matters.
- Many times, we feel that we are more important than others (remember the "EGO" discussion from *Law of EGO*?), hence why should we listen?
- Many times, we feel we know better the things that are the subject of the discussion. So, why should we listen? Again our "EGO" friend comes into discussion… I remember an old quote (sorry that I do not recall the author): "little knowledge is dangerous, but more knowledge can be even more dangerous". So true…
- Naturally, we think faster than the other talk, hence we need to fill the time and our thoughts drift away and we lose attention

- We may fear to talk and, awaiting our turn, we get blocked because of this freight. And we do not listen anymore...

So far, we have looked at some potential reasons why it is difficult to listen effectively. Now let us turn our focus on the different types of ineffective listening. Anybody dares to take the quiz: "how many of the below do you usually do?" I got 6 out of 6... You?

- **Aggressive listening**: it happens usually when we are forced to listen, and we do not want to, for example when we are sent to a meeting where we do not want to be, but we still have to listen and take notes.
- **Passive listening**: we do not want to talk, so we have no other choice but to listen to the speaker who talks endlessly.
- **Interrupted listening**: we want to talk, and we try to find a good moment to stop the other party from talking. It is very interesting when both parties are in the same mode!
- **Logical listening**: this is rational listening (with the brains only), without involving the understanding of nonverbal messages. It often leads to passive or aggressive listening.
- **Arrogant listening**: this is a very passive, egocentric way of listening. We feel extremely comfortable, in a relaxed posture, maybe with our feet on the desk, looking at the ceiling or the floor, etc. I had a colleague in P&G who had this attitude. He was always full of himself in meetings with agencies and took all the opportunities to show off how strong and good he is. I tried to explain to him that "he should not get drunk with plain water and be humbler", but he never wanted to take my advice.
- **Nervous listening**: this is very often encountered in stressful situations; meeting with the direct boss, recruiting interviews, TV interviews, etc. You can recognize it by the

nervous gestures of the person involved, his sweating, and his requests to repeat information.

Good, so far so clear, but how can we listen effectively? I prepared for you a few recommendations, based on my experience:

- First, **decide to listen effectively**. This means you must consciously go through the following sequence of steps:
    o Listen => think => take a pause => take a deep breath => speak
- **Block all judgment**. Stop judging the other party until he finished speaking. It is so easy to jump to conclusions halfway through the speech of the other party. Believe me, I lived many such episodes in my career, with colleagues of mine who would not let me finish my phrases and jump to the wrong conclusions (usually becoming extremely aggressive). It would then take me 5 minutes to calm them down and ask them to shut up until I finish.
- **Check for understanding**. It is so easy to misunderstand a message... and jump to the wrong conclusion. Therefore, always try to paraphrase what you have been told and make sure you got the right message.
- **Use a positive non-verbal language**. Always keep in mind that in communication, 10% of the effect is because of words, 35% because of tone and phrasing, and 55% because of the non-verbal language.
- **Use words to show understanding of what has been said and the interest in the subject**
- **Use and appreciate silence**. W. A. Mozart said: "silence is the most profound sound in music". Use it to digest the information! Also, a strategic silence during a tough negotiation often makes the counterparty feel uncomfortable and might allow them to break a negotiation deadlock.

5. Summarizing

This is a particularly important trait of the Elite Negotiator™ because it helps move forward the negotiation. How so? From time to time during a lengthier negotiation and always at the end of a negotiation meeting, summarize all that was said and agreed. When doing so, ask the other party for approval on every point and ask for feedback. If you get feedback, incorporate it on the spot and summarize again that point. Only after you get the approval of the other party that your summary is accurate, move to the other point.

In a regular negotiation meeting, my recommendation is to summarize each negotiation point once you get to a conclusion and always before the breaks. Upon returning from break, read again the summary to make sure everybody is on the same wavelength.

If you finish a negotiation in one single meeting, then you just need to do the final summary, after all the points have been discussed. Then you prepare a written summary of the discussion, covering all that was discussed and agreed, and send it to the other party for the record.

My advice is that YOU do all the summaries (intermediary, as well as the final summary). It is not because you plan to cheat the other party! By no means! It is just easier for you to follow the negotiation step by step and point by point, given that you do the summaries. And, in this way, you make sure no mistakes get in…

I think I cannot stress enough the importance of the summary of what has been agreed so far. Recently, in a session of my 3-days highly intensive "Elite Negotiator™" training, during one of the easy negotiation simulations (a pretty straightforward buyer-seller negotiation), the two players ended the negotiation without summarizing what they finally agreed. And because of this omission, the buyer had one understanding, while the seller had a hugely different one (the "gap" being a significant amount of money). The two discovered this only when we debriefed after the exercise – and then the seller said there is no deal because he is not going to implement the agreement as such (the seller being at a loss). It was the perfect real example (and an enormously powerful one for everybody watching) that a simple step like "summarizing" can be a deal killer if we do not do it properly.

Real story

I remember one meeting I had with a very large multinational manufacturer (let us call it "Mega Producer"), who asked us to partner in a trade marketing program.

I am a very open-minded guy (at least I want to believe so...) and I said yes, hence we met the sales and trade marketing team of the Mega Producer. The meeting was very interesting, took almost 3 hours and we aligned on a draft implementation plan. At the end of the meeting, I made the mistake of letting the trade marketing manager of Mega Producer write the summary.

In a couple of days, we got the summary, which, to our shock, included elements that we never agreed! It was a pure and simple lie! We would have never expected from such a huge multinational company to behave so unethically. I went mad and reverted to them with my strong comments and amendments.

> Finally, the plan was implemented as discussed in the meeting, but I took my big learning about who should do the summary.
>
> And my second learning was regarding the ethical behavior of the representatives of Mega Producer. I was never able to trust that company again, even if it was one individual who did the unethical move....

In negotiations that do not finish in one single meeting, do the intermediary summary at the end of the day, and send it to all participants, requesting feedback. Even if you did your clarification and summarizing job brilliantly, be prepared that the other party may revert to you saying that one or several points were not agreed as per your summary. I know it is abnormal to happen, especially if you did your job and aligned everything. But, trust me, I went through this much more often than you think… Yes, it was shocking to me as well…

I will give you another real-life example:

> ### Real story
>
> For almost one year, we were unable to finalize the negotiations with a marketing agency for an important project. The agency had a very consistent behavior of altering the agreements reached in our face to face meetings once they arrived at their headquarters. They were doing it in a very "slippery" way and always with the attitude "Yes, but what we really meant was… for sure it was a misunderstanding, but we cannot accept that point". And on and on again. In the end, we always had some points that had to be renegotiated, allegedly because of the misunderstanding. You can imagine how frustrating the whole relationship was…

I hope you could see that indeed, achieving communication excellence is not a simple task. But, if there is a will, I am sure there will be a way, and, should you decide to respect this Immutable Law, you will reap the benefits extremely fast!

+1.

THE LAW OF *REALITY CHECK*

Always check if your deal passes the most important test: sustainability in implementation!

This law is a very special one for me, personally, because I broke it many times, especially at the beginning of my career and I paid the price for it. Let me share with you just two personal, bitter experiences:

> **Real story**
>
> At the time of this story I was responsible for the key Point of Market Entry Programs of Procter & Gamble (Always Educational Program, respectively Pampers Hospital Program and Direct Mailing) across all Balkan countries.
>
> A significant part of the budget we spent was on printed materials that we gave away to the people in the target group together with the product samples. In my quest of cost optimization, I organized a tender for printing all the materials in Romania for all programs, for all countries. That was a megatender, never done before! I was "young and fearless", so I was optimistic that I could make it work from a logistics point of view AND make a hefty saving in the process. Truth be told,

I had a bit of experience with the printed materials tender, as I did one for the same programs (but only for one country) in the previous year.

I did my Due Diligence properly and only invited reputable companies, with turnover significantly larger than the project value. All had extremely good reputation on the market in terms of reliability. All stars looked quite "aligned" for what was supposed to be a super successful tender.

The tender was indeed very competitive and in the shortlist the battle was fierce. In the end, one company ("Maxi Printer") won the tender. I started meeting with their representatives on a weekly basis to check the status of the printing.

But, what started well, turned out to be bitter in the end! To be honest, I was lucky that the Sales Director of another printing company taught me the secret of finding out if a printing company cheats you (or not) by checking the specific weight of the paper they used. The "neophytes" estimate the specific weight by touching the paper between two fingers, by trying to feel how thick it is: they believe that thickness is proportional with the specific weight! TOTALLY WRONG! For example, the same 90g/sqm paper can be denser, therefore it can feel thinner than a more voluminous paper with the same specific weight. Therefore, the only way to properly check the specific weight is by using a special weighting scale for paper and carton.

Having this information and having purchased a special scale, once I got the samples of all the printed materials produced by "Maxi Printer", I immediately checked their specific weights. To my surprise, 2 of the brochures were printed on lower paper weight (on 70g/sqm vs the required 80g/sqm). It was virtually impossible to feel the difference between the two types of paper by simply touching them, therefore if it were not for the scale, I would have not noticed the cheat.

I met "Maxi Printer" and showed them the evidence. Their disclaimer was the fact that they gave us exceptionally low prices which, later, they could not support anymore.

Obviously, I renegotiated the costs for those brochures, but I made sure we never worked with "Maxi Printer" again, given their lack of business ethics.

Above all, **my key learning was to check how realistic are the prices that I am getting in tenders**! Because, like I said this earlier in the book, "if something is too good to be true, then it is, indeed, too good to be true!"

In the following, second experience that I am sharing, bitter as well, I was not so lucky to have the advice of a more experienced person like in the case of "Maxi Printer":

Real story

I was working in as Marketing Director in the retail division of Metro Group, and I was planning the Anniversary campaign in one of the years. I ran a tender to appoint the agency that would ship the prizes to the shoppers that would win at our special raffle.

After the proper selection process, we appointed the winner (let us call it "The Smart Agency") that had the lowest price for the required tasks. All well, until we started receiving phone calls from disgruntled shoppers, terribly upset that they never received the prizes they won. We immediately checked with "The Smart Agency", which confirmed that they did not ship all the prizes, as they should have done. Their answer to our

> question why it takes them so long, their reply was startling: "at these low rates we are charging you, what do you expect: instant delivery?" I was speechless! They had the audacity to say that we should have not expected them to deliver as per the brief, simply because they quoted very low prices!
>
> We involved the Legal department and forced them to deliver as per the requirements. But our shoppers were terribly disappointed by how WE treated them (they considered, rightfully so, that it was OUR fault that they did not get their prizes on time).
>
> My learning here is similar like in the first example: **check how realistic/how feasible are the prices you get quoted!**

I am a chemical engineer, so I like chemical tests: for me, the "litmus test" for any deal is

whether or not what had been agreed in the negotiation fully survives the implementation phase

So, do not get happy too early at the sight of an incredibly good deal! Check for its realism in the implementation phase. **You may end up having an overall much more expensive deal if you squeeze the other party beyond what is reasonable, and you do not get delivered what you need!**

I can sense your question: "but what's reasonable"? To answer this question, you must do your proper homework and understand the market for what you are buying, as well as your historical buying prices. If what you get quoted now is significantly different vs market and/or versus what you bought previously, then beware and check again the offer for realism!

MY CHALLENGE TO YOU, THE READER!

Dear reader, I have shared with you, in this book, my **10+1 paramount learnings what one MUST DO to win any negotiation.** As said, they stem from my 20+ years of international business negotiation experience. They served me extremely well, each time I applied them, but also "penalized" me each time I did not. That is why I dared to call them **"Immutable Laws"**.

However, as all people are different, the same holds for negotiations. There are no two identical negotiations! Not even when the two parties are the same! To give you just one example, when I was Media Manager in P&G, I negotiated for many years with the same Director of a publishing house. One might think that the negotiations were quite similar over the years, especially as we knew each other well. They were not! Each year there were changes in the key parameters: business background, market, our needs, their strategy, our competitors' activity, their competitors' activity, etc. So, while we ended up having excellent deals each year, the negotiations were different.

The above being said **I decided to raise a challenge to you, dear reader!** A challenge that will benefit us both!

> I am challenging you to put these 10+1 Laws at work immediately and share with me:
> **1. how well they worked for you and what improvement suggestions you have for me as far as the Laws are concerned**
> **2. your real-life stories based on your own negotiations, after applying these Laws**

Your feedback will be highly appreciated, as it will help me improve this book going further. Also, I will publish the best real-life examples received, that use these Laws, in future editions of this book!

Please kindly send me your feedback and examples via email at <u>eugen.mihai@theelitenegotiator.com</u>

THANK YOU VERY MUCH for helping develop new generations of Elite Negotiators across the World!

"THE ELITE NEGOTIATOR™"
SHORT NEGO PREPARATION PLAN

© *Eugeniu D. Mihai 2014-2020*

Plan your dive and dive your plan!

SCUBA DIVERS' MOTTO

- Details about who fills in the form and date:

Name & Surname: _____
Position in company: _____
Date of filling in: _____

- Who negotiates?

	Partner No. 1 *("YOU")*	*Partner No. 2* *("THEM")*
Company:		
Main representative - *Name /* *Surname* - *Position*		
Representative 2 - *Name /* *Surname* - *Position*		
Representative 3 - *Name /* *Surname* - *Position*		

- What is the history of the relationship between the parties? Detail outcome of previous negotiations & any watch-outs.

_____
_____
_____

- **Why negotiating?**

	YOU	**THEM**
Is there a NEED or a WANT for the deal?		
Why each party enters the negotiation?		
What each party can lose if the negotiation fails?		
How can each party HELP the other?		
How can each party "HURT" the other?		

- **What are the interests, positions, and motivators for each party? Remember the "iceberg theory"!**

	YOU	**THEM**
Interests / issues		
Positions		
Motivators: • *Material* • *Psychological / personality*		

Mark / underline the interests, positions, and motivators where you feel it will be difficult to get to an agreement.

- **What are the negotiation subjects and the limits for each point to be negotiated?**

No.	Point to negotiate	Deal breaker (Y/N)	Min. acceptable	Ideal	Most likely	To give up (concession)
1.						
2.						
3.						

4.					
5.					
6.					

- **What are the alternatives if the negotiation fails?**

Alternative	YOU	THEM
1.		
2.		
3.		

If YOU do not have an alternative for this negotiation, then you MUST create at least one!
Try to estimate the alternatives for the other party: are there alternatives for your goods or services? How can you make your service or product UNIQUE vis-à-vis our negotiation partner, such that they will want to close the deal with you?

_____

_____

- **Analysis of the market positioning:**

What are the most recent trends on the market and how are they influencing the two negotiation parties?

Trend	Influence on YOU	Influence on THEM
1.		
2.		
3.		
4.		

- **Estimating the POWER level of each party**

How can you maximize YOUR power level and counteract THEIR power sources? Write below the sources of your and their power

Source of power	Level YOU (W / M / S*)	Level THEM (W / M / S*)

- **Which are the STRONG and WEAK points of the two negotiation parties? Summarize all info collected so far!**

	YOU	*THEM*
Strengths 1. 2. 3. 4. 5.		
Weaknesses 1. 2. 3. 4. 5.		

- What tactics YOU will use in the negotiation and how THEY can counteract them? What tactics will THEY most likely employ and how can you defend against them?

*Remember the 6 questions **Acid test for using the negotiation tactics** before deciding what tactic to use!*

	Tactics	YOU		THEM	
		How to use?	How can be neutralized?	How will they use it?	How can be neutralized?
1					
2					
3					
4					
5					

ABOUT THE AUTHOR

Eugeniu D. Mihai is the founder of "The Elite Negotiator™" book and highly intensive training program that benefited thousands on 4 continents since its launch in 2016, and that is considered to be **"the most effective and interactive negotiation training on the market"** by the participants.

Eugeniu holds a Master of Science in Industrial Organic Chemistry from "Politehnica" University of Bucharest, Valedictorian, class of 1996.

He has over 24 years of business management experience in a multinational FMCG company (Procter & Gamble), in a major international retail chain (METRO Group AG, retail division), in a leading full-service advertising agency, specialized in consumer engagement (Wave Division Group).

Most recently, he was the CEO of one of Europe's largest angel investor networks specialized in financing early-stage businesses (Angels Den Funding Limited UK), respectively the Cluster Procurement Director at Molson Coors Romania & Bulgaria.

Since 1998 Eugeniu D. Mihai has been intensively involved in hundreds of national and international business negotiations for the companies he worked for. He had also been requested to counsel and represent various business people in their negotiations.

Eugeniu D. Mihai is an officially qualified and awarded trainer of "Negotiation and Influencing Skills" and a Professor of "Business Strategy" and "Managerial Finance" at the Romanian International Advertisers Association School of Marketing & Communication.

Among the companies that benefited from Eugeniu's various negotiation training can be mentioned: Procter & Gamble,

British American Tobacco, Molson Coors, Fine Hygienic Holding, Leo Burnett, SAB Miller / Asahi, McCann Ericsson, Papyrus Europe, EXL, Saatchi & Saatchi, Kubis Interactive, CEO Clubs International Europe, International Advertisers Association – Romanian Chapter, Business Women Forum Romania, Flanco Retail, Profi Supermarkets, Hartmann Medical, Zenith Optimedia, CERES Labor Union, Tarus Media, Ax Perpetuum, etc.

"The Elite Negotiator™" program includes:
- An array of training (1, 2 or 3 days, customizable)
- LIVE Webinars and on-demand keynote speeches on various negotiation topics
- Negotiation workshops (4 hours) – the most popular topics being "The biggest negotiation mistakes" and "The most effective negotiation strategies and tactics"

All types of "Elite Negotiation™" training can be run as "open" or "in-house". The "in-house" option is allowing customized, tailor-made content, maximizing the impact on the target audience. Also, over 70% of the time of the workshops and of the training is dedicated to negotiation exercises and simulations, with on-the-spot debriefing.

For inquiries about the "Elite Negotiation™" franchise or any other business training, LIVE Webinars or speeches, please email: Eugen.mihai@theelitenegotiator.com

More details on https://www.theelitenegotiator.com

www.ingramcontent.com/pod-product-compliance
Lightning Source LLC
Chambersburg PA
CBHW051536240526
45465CB00027B/272